Fiuza/MICHELIN

Hostal de los Reyes Católicos

1

A city of pilgrimage

14 Santiago, the city
   of the Apostle
18 The Apostle St James:
   history and tradition
20 The Way of St James
26 Pilgrimage rituals

Highlights

40 Cathedral

Introduction

4 Introduction
6 City map
8 General map
10 Location

Background

30 A city of water
32 "Tuna" music groups
34 Local gastronomy
36 Handicrafts and souvenirs

Exploring the city

48 From plaza del Obradoiro
   to plaza de la Quintana
54 From plaza de la Universitad
   to plaza de Cervantes
58 From plaza de Cervantes
   to plaza del Obradoiro

Museums and sights of interest

64 Museums
68 Other places of interest
70 Places of interest around Santiago

Excursions

74 A Coruña / La Coruña
80 Lugo
84 Ourense / Orense
87 Around Ourense / Orense
90 Pontevedra
94 Rías Altas
100 Rías Bajas

Directory

120 Transport
120 Sightseeing
121 Where to Eat
123 Tapas
123 Where to Stay
125 Bars and Cafés

Index

126

In the Middle Ages, Santiago de Compostela, the third most important city of pilgrimage after Jerusalem and Rome, attracted pilgrims from all over Europe. According to the German poet Goethe, walking the ways of St James to Santiago awakened the "European conscience".

It remains one of Spain's most enchanting cities with its magnificent monumental centre and maze of narrow streets which were declared a UNESCO World Heritage Site in 1984. Contrary to all expectations, however, the styles of architecture that predominate here are Baroque and neo-Classical, rather than Romanesque, lending an air of solemnity to the city, a sensation that can be best appreciated from the paseo de la Herradura.

It is also a lively city, a reputation enhanced by its numerous bars and taverns, thousands of university students, and the throng of annual visitors. And with its artistic and musical heritage, its traditions and its history, Santiago has something for everyone.

Introduction

Cathedral façade

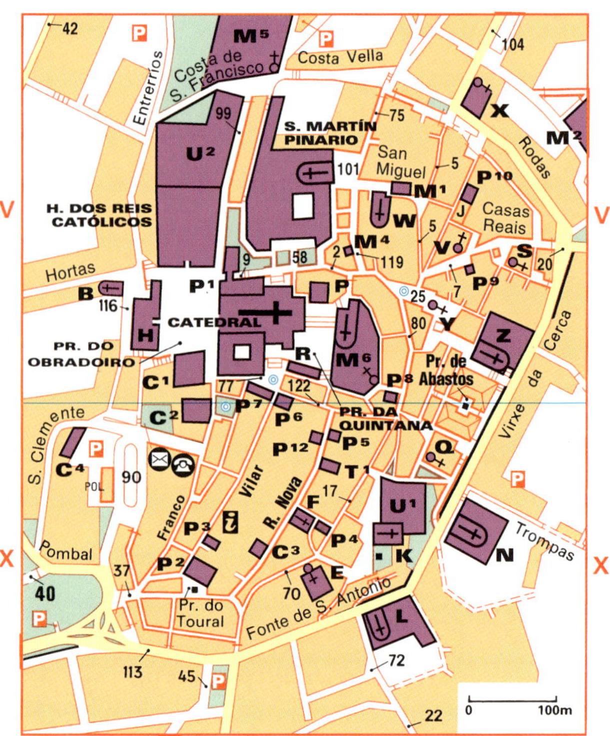

Acibechería............................ **V** 2
Algalia de Arriba................... **V** 5
Ánimas .... **V** 7
Arco de Palacio .... **V** 9
Caldeirería............................ **X** 17
Camiño (Porta do)................. **V** 20
Castrón Douro....................... **X** 22
Cervantes (Pr. De)............... **V** 25
Faxeiras (Porta da)............... **X** 37
Ferradura (Pas. Da).............. **X** 40
Galeras .... **V** 42
Galicia (Pr. De)..................... **X** 45
Immaculada (Pr. Da) .... **V** 58
Nova (R.)............................... **X**
Orfas.................................... **X** 70
Patio de Madres.................... **X** 72
Pena (Porta de la) .... **V** 75
Praterías (Pr. Das)............... **V** 77
Preguntoiro .... **V** 80
Rodrigo de Padrón (Av. de) . **X** 90
San Francisco........................ **V** 99
San Martíño (Pr. De)............. **V** 101
San Roque .... **V** 104
Senra .... **X** 113
Trinidade............................... **V** 116
Troia .... **V** 119
Vilar (R. do) .... **X**
Xelmírez................................ **VX** 122

Antigua iglesia de la Compañía .... **X K**
Antiguo colegio dos Irlandeses.................. **X C³**
Antiguo hospital e iglesia de San Roque .... **V X**
Ayuntamiento (Pazo de Raxoi)............... **V H**
Casa da Conga.................... **V R**
Casa das Pomas .... **X P¹²**
Casa de la Parra.................. **V P**
Casa del Cabildo............. **VX P⁷**
Casa do Déan.................... **VX P⁶**
Casa-Museo da Troia .... **V M⁴**
Casa-pazo de Vaamonde.. **X P³**
Casa-pazo dos Fonseca.... **X P⁴**

Centro Galego de Arte
    Contemporánea .... V M²
Colegio
    de San Clemente............. X C⁴
Colegio
    de San Jerónimo............ V C¹
Colegio Fonseca .... VX C²
Convento de San Francisco
    (Museo de Terra Santa) . Y M⁵
Convento del Colegio
    de la Compañía
    de María .... X N
Convento e iglesia de las
    Madres Mercedarias ...... X L
Convento e iglesia
    de San Agustín .... V Z
Facultad de Medicina .... V U²
Iglesia das Ánimas .... V V
Iglesia de San Benito
    del Campo .... V Y
Iglesia de San Fiz
    de Solovio........................ X Q
Iglesia de San Fructuoso .. V B

Iglesia de San Miguel
    dos Agros .... V W
Iglesia de Santa María
    del Camino .... V S
Iglesia de Santa
    María Salomé.................... X F
Iglesia y colegio
    das Orfas.......................... X E
Monasterio de San Paio
    de Antealtares
    (Museo de Arte Sacra)... V M⁶
Museo de las
    Peregrinaciones.............. V M¹
Palacio Gelmírez
    (Pazo de Xelmírez) .... V P¹
Pazo de Amarante............. V P¹⁰
Pazo de Bendaña (Fundación
    Eugenio Granell).............. X P²
Pazo de Feijoo................... V P⁸
Pazo de Fondevila .... V P⁹
Pazo de Santa Cruz........... X P⁵
Teatro Principal .... X T¹
Universidad........................ X U¹

Parque de la Música

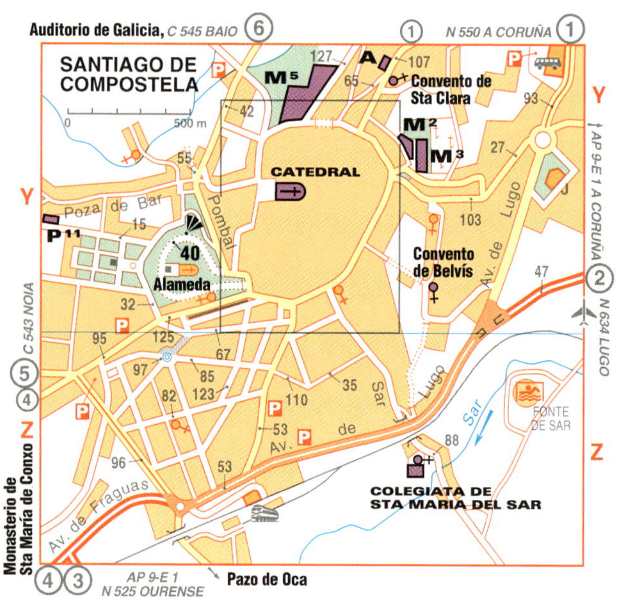

Burgás (Av. das)................... Y 15
Concheiros .... Y 27
Coruña (Av. da)................... Y 32
Curros Enríquez .... Z 35
Ferradura (Pas. Da)............. Y 40
Galeras .... Y 42
Gonzalo Torrente
  Ballester (Av.) .... Y 47
Hórrero .... Z 53
Hortas (Campo das)............ Y 55
Loureiros .... Y 65
Montero Ríos .... YZ 67
República Arxentina .... Z 82

República de
  El Salvador...................... Z 85
Rodiño (Corredoira)............ Z 88
Rodríguez de Viguri .... Y 93
Romero Donallo .... Z 96
Rosalía de Castro (Av. de)..Z 95
Roxa (Pr.) .... Z 97
San Pedro .... Y 103
Santa Clara .... Y 107
Santiago de Guayaquil ...... Z 110
Xeneral Pardiñas .... Z 123
Xoán Carlos I (Av.) .... YZ 125
Xoán XXIII (Av. de)............. Y 127

Centro Galego de Arte
  Contemporánea .... Y M²
Convento del Carmen ...... Y A
Convento de San Francisco
  (Museo de Terra Santa) Y M⁵

Museo do Pobo
  Galego .... Y M³
Pazo de San Lourenzo
  de Trasouto .... Y P¹¹

Detail, Cathedral

Population: 105 851. Michelin map 571 D 4._ This important pilgrimage city enjoys a strategic location at the heart of Galicia. It stands at the junction of several main roads, including the AP 9, linking it with Pontevedra (57km/35.5mi S), Vigo (84km/52.5mi S) and A Coruña/La Coruña (72km/45mi N), the N 547, running east to Lugo (107km/67mi), and the AP 53, heading southeast to Ourense (111km/69mi). The city's airport is located at Km 11 along the Santiago-Lugo road (N 547), while the train station is just a couple of minutes' drive to the southwest of the historical centre.

Santiago's historic buildings, narrrow streets and delightful parks are best explored on foot. This is compulsory for the city's old quarter, which is entirely pedestrianised, with motorists having to park at one of several car parks outside the monumental centre.

Vilar 63, 15705, ☎ 981 55 51 29; plaza de Galicia, 15706, ☎ 981 57 39 90.

J. Fiuza/MICHELIN

Location

A city of pilgrimage

Santiago, the city of the Apostle

The delightful city of Santiago de Compostela grew up around the tomb of the Apostle St James, discovered here in the 9C. By the Middle Ages the city had already become one of the capital cities of Christianity, along with Rome and Jerusalem, and the destination of millions of pilgrims who set out from the most remote corners of Europe on long, arduous journies to venerate the Apostle.

However, Santiago is much more than just an important religious city. It has a university tradition that dates back centuries, which is partly responsible for its lively atmosphere and the wide range of cultural activities on offer. Capital of the Comunidad Autónoma de Galicia since 1980, the city has the added attraction of a magnificent historical centre, which was declared a UNESCO World Heritage Site in 1984 and acts as an international stage for visitors from around the world.

The medieval city

After the discovery of the Apostle's tomb at the beginning of the 9C, a simple church was built to house the mausoleum. This church was replaced at the end of the century by a pre-Romanesque-style basilica, which at the time was the largest on the Iberian peninsula, testimony to the importance of the pilgrimage here since its earliest days.

At the end of the 10C, Almanzor arrived in Galicia and razed both the town and the church; both were subsequently rebuilt and the new church was consecrated at the beginning of the 11C. The town continued to grow and towards the middle of the 11C fortifications were built marking out the boundary of the present historic centre. Around 1075, Maestro Bernardo el Viejo was entrusted with the task of building a large Romanesque cathedral.

In 1099, the bishopric passed to **Diego Gelmírez**, a key figure in the history of Santiago. He appointed Maestro Esteban to continue with work on the cathedral, which was completed in 1125, and oversaw the construction of the Bishop's Palace and other churches in the town. Santiago continued to thrive and by the time of Gelmírez's death in 1140, it could be said that the medieval city was largely finished.

In 1168, Maestro Mateo was appointed to build two important architectural features in the cathedral: the Pórtico de la Gloria and the choir. The Pórtico de la Gloria is without doubt one of the most important works of art of all time. Unfortunately, the equally impressive choir has not survived, although some of its magnificent reliefs now adorn the Puerta Santa.

The 13C was of major importance for Santiago, with the consecration of the cathedral taking place in 1211. By this time, the Camino Francés (also known as the Camino de Santiago, or Way of St James) was clearly established, substantially increasing the number of pilgrims making their way to the city. Trade flourished as a result and the city experienced a period of urban growth with the establishment of several mendicant orders outside the city walls. The monasteries of San Francisco, Santa María de Bonaval and Santa Clara were subsequently founded.

J. Fiuza/MICHELIN

Rúa do Vilar

Santiago during the Renaissance

During the 16C, a period which was dominated by the Plateresque style, several important architectural changes took place in the city, especially in the public areas around the cathedral; these changes were only finally completed during the Baroque period. The Hospital Real, funded by the Catholic Kings, was built at this time, as was plaza de Platerías, laid out on the site of the cathedral's Romanesque cloisters. This period also saw the construction of the Monasterio de San Paio Antealtares, whose wide side wall flanks the plaza de Quintana; the Colegio Fonseca, home to the University; and the church of the Monasterio de San Martín Pinario.

Baroque transformation

During the second half of the 17C and the 18C, Santiago gradually acquired its present-day appearance. The Baroque architectural style became dominant in the city as many new buildings were constructed and older structures transformed. The cathedral saw the addition of the Puerta Real, which leads into plaza de Quintana, the north façade, known as the Fachada de la Azabachería, the spectacular façade of the Obradoiro, designed by Fernando Casas y Novoa, and the dome. New buildings in plaza de la Quintana included Casa de la Parra and Casa de la Conga, while in plaza del Obradoiro, the Classical style was already evident in the architecture of the Palacio de Raxoi. The University was built at the end of the 18C in neo-Classical style.

The modern city

Santiago received a new lease of life when the institutions of the autonomous region of Galicia were moved here following the city's declaration as regional capital in 1980. Recent years have seen the construction of emblematic buildings such as the Auditorio de Galicia, designed by Julio Cano Lasso; the Centro Galego de Arte Contemporáneo, by the renowned Portuguese architect Álvaro Siza, who was also responsible for the remodelling of the old cemetery in Parque de San Domingos de Bonaval; and the Palacio de Congresos y Exposiciones, the work of Alberto Noguerol. These buildings are a clear sign of the vitality of a city which is open to change and which looks back at its past with pride, while facing its future with confidence.

Santiago Cathedral

17

© Jaffres/MICHELIN

The Apostle St James: history and tradition

According to legend, the Apostle St James crossed the seas to preach in "Finis Terrae" (literally "the Ends of the Earth" – this name has evolved today into the province of Finisterre). His boat was cast ashore at the mouth of the River Ulla and he preached for seven years before returning to Palestine where he was decapitated by Herod Agrippa. His disciples were forced to flee the Holy Land and returned to Spain with his body, which they buried in Iria Flavia, erecting a marble tomb and an altar in his honour.

However, the passing of time, which saw subsequent invasions by the Barbarians and later the Arabs, caused the grave to be lost to memory.

At the beginning of the 9C, the hermit Pelayo is said to have been guided to the grave in the Librédon wood by a shower of stars. Surprised at what he had seen, Pelayo related this strange event to the bishop of Iria Flavia, Teodomiro, who, upon arriving at the wood, discovered the

J. Fiuza/MICHELIN

tomb holding the apostle's remains.

The discovery of necropoli beneath the cathedral seems to support the theory that the word Compostela derives from a word in vulgar Latin meaning "a place of burial", rather than from *campus stellae* or "field of stars".

In 844, Don Ramiro I was leading a handful of Spaniards in a bold attack against the Moors grouped at **Clavijo** near Logroño when a knight in armour, mounted on a charger and bearing a white standard with a red cross upon it, is said to have appeared on the battlefield. As he beat back the infidels the Christians recognised St James, naming him from that time *Matamoros* or Slayer of the Moors. The Reconquest and Spain had found a patron saint. During the crusade, it is said that one of the Christian leaders, the Lord of Pimentel, had to swim across a *ría*. He emerged from the sea covered in shells which were then adopted as the pilgrims' symbol.

In the IIC devotion spread abroad until a journey to St James' shrine ranked equally with one to Rome or Jerusalem, particularly perilous since the invasion of the Holy Land by the Turks. St James had a particular appeal for the French who felt united with the Spanish in the face of the Moorish threat, but English, Germans, Italians and even Scandinavians made the long pilgrimage, travelling for the most part through France along the routes organised to a considerable degree by the Benedictines and Cistercians of Cluny and Cîteaux.

Padrón, where St James' body was brought ashore

The way of St James

The discovery of the body of the Apostle James in Santiago de Compostela transformed this city into the most important pilgrimage centre in Europe during the Middle Ages. From the 11C onwards, the veneration of relics – a fundamental feature of religious devotion during this period – gave rise to the development of a path that led to this Galician city, where pilgrims could worship the body of the Apostle.

Today, thousands of pilgrims continue to walk the Way of St James (Camino de Santiago), and although for some at least the journey has lost its religious significance, it provides an opportunity to explore the history and culture of this fascinating part of the Iberian Peninsula.

The origins and development of the Way of St James

The relics of St James (Santiago) discovered early in the 9C soon became the object of a local cult and then of pilgrimage. In the 11C, devotion spread abroad until a journey to St James' shrine ranked equally with one to Rome or Jerusalem.

Every year, half a million pilgrims from across Western Europe embarked (and continue to embark) upon their journey to Santiago de Compostela in the traditional pilgrim's **"uniform"** comprising a broad-brimmed felt hat, heavy cape to combat the cold, stave (large stick), gourd to carry water, and the infamous scallop shell. In bygone days, these pilgrimages represented the main cultural medium through which new European cultural trends (eg Romanesque art, Provençal lyrical poetry etc) arrived in Spain; they also enabled the dissemination across Europe of new ideas from the Iberian Peninsula.

The Benedictines of Cluny established an organisation to help those pilgrims undertaking this arduous journey, the Knights Templar and the Spanish Order of the Red Sword assured the pilgrims' safety, provided them with funds and flagged the route with cairns, and the Hospitallers set up hospitals and hospices to care for the sick. A Pilgrim Guide of 1130, the first tourist guide ever written, probably by Aimeri Picaud, a Poitou monk from Parthenay-le-Vieux, describes the inhabitants, climate and customs of different regions, the most interesting routes, and the sights on the way – the pilgrim in those days was in no hurry and frequently made detours to visit a sanctuary

J. Fiuza/MICHELIN

Iglesia de San Fiz, Santiago de Compostela

or shrine, many of which took weeks or months to complete.

The stopping places along the way formed a main street or **calle Mayor** around which a village would develop. Farming communities grew into towns and some were settled by foreigners or minority groups (often French, Jewish or Mudéjar) who consolidated the recovered territory and brought with them a wealth of culture.

The Wars of Religion dealt a serious blow for the pilgrimage route, severely reducing the numbers of those setting out for Santiago. Finally in 1589, Drake attacked La Coruña and the bishop of Compostela removed the relics from the cathedral to a place of safety; for 300 years the pilgrimage was virtually abandoned. However, in 1879 they were recovered, recognised by the Pope and the pilgrimage recommenced.

ONE PILGRIMAGE, SEVERAL ROUTES

All the information you are likely to need can be found at www.xacobeo.es or obtained from the Pilgrimage Information Office (Oficina de Información del Camino), rúa do Vilar, 30-32, Santiago de Compostela, ☏ 981 57 20 04.

Over the centuries, pilgrims reaching Santiago from the various corners of Europe followed routes that are still used today.

Camino Francés

This path was, and still is, the most important pilgrims' route, both in terms of the number of pilgrims and its artistic and cultural significance.

The various paths through France met at Roncesvalles, Behobia and Somport to cross the Pyrenees and continued through northeastern Spain along two routes – the Asturian, from Roncesvalles, which until the 15C was considered extremely dangerous because of possible attack by brigands, and a more southerly route from Somport, known as the **Camino Francés**, or French Way, on account of the number of French pilgrims who followed it. It became marked over the centuries by churches and monasteries in which French architectural influence is obvious. The two routes converged at Puente la Reina.

The main stopping-points from Somport to Puente la Reina were Jaca, Santa Cruz de la Serós, San Juan de la Peña, the Monasterio de Leyre and Sangüesa. The route from Roncesvalles to Puente la Reina was the shorter of the two with only one main stop at Pamplona/Iruña.

From Puente la Reina, the French Way continued along a single route which passed by a number of important settlements before entering Galicia via the O Cebreiro pass. The important sites and towns along its path included the Iglesia de Santa María de Eunate, Cirauqui, Estella, the Monasterio de Irache, Los Arcos, the Iglesia del Santa Sepulcro de Torres del Río, Nájera, Santo Domingo de la

J. Fiuza/MICHELIN

Detail, door of the Colegio de San Jerónimo, Santiago de Compostela

23

Calzada, Burgos, the Iglesia de San Martín de Frómista, Villalcázar de Sirga, Carrión de los Condes, León, Astorga and Ponferrada.

Camino del Norte

The North Way, like the Original Way (Camino Primitivo), was of major importance during the early pilgrimages to the area. This route followed the coast of the old kingdom of Asturias and entered Galicia at Ribadeo by crossing the river from Castropol.

From the 11C and 12C, the North Way gradually lost its importance as the French Way grew in popularity.

Camino Primitivo

As its name suggests, the Original Way was the route used by the very first pilgrims setting out from Oviedo to visit the Apostle's tomb. This much-frequented route was eventually overtaken in popularity by the French Way passing through León, a city which was to replace Oviedo as the new capital of the Asturian kingdom.

Camino Inglés

The English Way was the name given to the route followed by pilgrims travelling from the British Isles and Scandinavia, who embarked at the ports of A Coruña/La Coruña or El Ferrol, and then made their way on foot to Santiago (74km/46mi from A Coruña/La Coruña and 118km/74mi from El Ferrol).

Camino Portugués

The Portuguese Way entered Galicia at Tui by crossing the River Miño. This pilgrims' route grew in popularity from the 12C and helped to forge important cultural and economic ties between Portugal and Galicia.

Camino del Sudeste – Via de la Plata

This route, known as the Southeast Way, was used by pilgrims from the central and southern sections of the Iberian Peninsula, passing through Mérida and entering Galicia through the province of Orense.

For much of its length it followed the Silver Route, the old Roman road that crossed the western half of the Iberian peninsula from north to south. Pilgrims could follow the Roman road as far as Astorga and then meet up with the French Way or take a detour to Puebla de Sanabria. This route spends the largest amount of time in Galicia, crossing the region through the provinces of Orense, Pontevedra and A Coruña/La Coruña.

Camino de Fisterra

This route is considered to be one of the Ways of St James, although many of the pilgrims following it to Santiago would then continue to Finisterre (Fisterra) which, as its names suggests, was for centuries the end of the known world.

Ruta del Mar de Arousa y Río Ulla

According to tradition, this was the route by which the remains of the Apostle were taken to Santiago.

Fiuza/MICHELIN

Iglesia de San Fructuoso, Santiago de Compostela

Pilgrimage rituals

Pilgrims arrive in Santiago after a journey marked by physical hardship, yet with their hearts full of hope and joy. Their visit to the city's cathedral is largely governed by pre-established ritual.

In Holy Years access to the church is through the Puerta Santa. Once inside the cathedral, pilgrims make their way to the chapel of the high altar where they give the Apostle the traditional, emotional embrace. They then descend to the crypt where the remains of the Saint are kept. This is followed by a visit to the Pórtico de la Gloria in order to touch the slender mullion column and knock their head on the "Santo dos Croques", situated on the rear base of the column; this traditional rite is said to convey intelligence and wisdom from the saint to the pilgrim. It is also customary for the pilgrim to attend the Pilgrim's Mass, which takes place at noon.

The Compostela

The Compostela is the certificate awarded by the cathedral of Santiago in recognition of a pilgrimage made to the city. It is granted to all pilgrims who follow the Way of St James for religious reasons. In order to qualify for the certificate, pilgrims must complete a minimum of 100km/62mi on foot or on horseback, or 200km/124mi by bike, along one of the recognised routes. On arrival in Santiago, pilgrims may request the Compostela by presenting their pilgrim's card to the **Oficina del Peregrino** *(rúa do Vilar, I, ☎ 981 56 24 19)*. This pilgrim's card is a type of route book that must be signed or stamped by parishes, pilgrims' hostels etc at each of the official stages along the route.

Holy Year and Jubilee

A Holy Year in Santiago is one in which the feast day of St James (25 July) falls on a Sunday. This happens every 6, 5, 6 and 11 years. The next Holy Year is 2010.

During Holy Year, ceremonies in Santiago are particularly solemn and pilgrims are able to obtain the Jubilee, a full indulgence granted by the Church. In order to earn this, pilgrims must fulfil the following requirements: embark upon a pilgrimage to Santiago in order to pray before the Apostle (it is not necessary to follow the Way, simply going to Santiago is enough); ask the Pope for his blessing, and take confession or communion at some time either two weeks before or after the pilgrimage.

Background

A city of water

It is impossible to think of Santiago de Compostela without thinking of water. Rain, a symbol of fertility, is one of the main features of this lively, open city, which has a mild climate and often cloudy skies. It is said that in Santiago "rain is art" and it is true that this inland city is at its most typical on rainy days, when the water seems to enhance the timeless beauty of its elegant buildings and old streets. When the rain stops, the city looks clean and bright in the light of day or golden-hued at nightfall, with the street lamps creating a magical atmosphere in the squares and alleyways of the old town. And although bright sunny weather is obviously always welcome, no visit to Santiago is complete without experiencing its historic centre in the rain.

J. Fiuza/MICHELIN

CLIMATE

Santiago enjoys an Atlantic climate with mild temperatures in winter and summer. During the coldest months, the temperature rarely falls below 7°C/45°F and in summer it is hardly ever hotter than 25°C/77°F. On average it rains in Santiago 140 days of the year, which means at least one day out of three; whatever you do, make sure you pack an umbrella and raincoat in readiness for your visit.

Rain is not the only water present in Santiago, as the delightful squares of the old city (Platerías, Fonseca, Toural, Cervantes etc) are embellished by picturesque fountains, each with its own history. Some of these have hidden messages, while others depict traditions. As an example, the Fuente de los Caballos in plaza de Platerías is adorned by a woman sitting on a sarcophagus and holding a star in each hand; it is said that this sculpture represents the two possible etymologies of the word "Compostela": a place of burial (sarcophagus) or a field of stars (*campo de estrellas*).

Fuente de los Caballos, Plaza de Platerías

Tuna music groups

Santiago has one of the oldest universities in Spain. It is impossible to imagine the city without its renowned seat of learning or the thousands of students who throng its streets on the way to lectures by day and crowd its bars at night. And it is impossible to mention Santiago and its university life without making reference to the *tuna* (student music group), an institution that is both old and contemporary, and both traditional and bohemian.

From "sopistas" to tunos

The distant origins of the student musicians or *tunos* date back to the Middle Ages when poor students known as *sopistas* would sing love songs or bawdy tunes in exchange for a plate of soup (hence their name, from the Spanish "sopa") or a few coins to help pay for their board and lodging or studies.

From the 16C, students were usually housed in different buildings depending on the subjects they were studying. Here they were taken under the wing of an older student who would introduce them to university life and protect them from any possible bullying. In some ways the *tuna* can be said to have inherited this tradition: present-day *tuna* aspirants, after taking an entrance test and becoming "beginners", have to undertake a period of apprenticeship (which can last up to a year) during which they are supervised by experienced members of the group. At the end of their apprenticeship they are awarded the much-coveted sash *(see below)* and become fully-fledged members of the *tuna*.

Tuna costume

The black tuna costume is typical of that worn by students in the 18C. It consists of a doublet, a kind of tight-fitting jacket worn over a white shirt with large cuffs and collar; one of two types of trousers, either plus fours or loose-fitting shorts worn with breeches; and either shoes or boots.

An important part of the costume which differs from group to group is the sash, the band of colour worn over the chest and which identifies the faculty (by the colour) and University (by the shield) of the *tuna*.

The final part of the costume is the cloak, which is also black and decorated with colourful shields and ribbons. The shields are those of the cities and countries that the group has visited. The ribbons bear loving inscriptions and are given to the *tunos* by women; these ribbons can be of any colour, although traditionally red is used by the *tuno's* girlfriend and white by his mother.

Tuna compostelana

This, one of the most famous songs in the entire *tuna* repertoire, is inspired by and written for Santiago's younger generations, with lyrics that encompass the themes of unrequited love, tradition, the city's university and its cathedral.

Pasa la tuna en Santiago
cantando muy quedo romances de amor
luego la noche en sus ecos
los cuela de ronda por todo balcón
Y allá en el templo del Apóstol Santo
una niña llora ante su patrón
porque la capa del tuno que adora
no lleva las cintas que ella le bordó
porque la capa de tuno que adora
no lleva las cintas que ella le bordó

Cuando la tuna te de serenata
no te enamores compostelana
que cada cinta que adorna mi capa
guarda un trocito de un corazón
Ay tra la la la la la la
no te enamores compostelana
y deja la tuna pasar
con su tra la la la la

Hoy va la tuna de gala
cantando y tocando la marcha nupcial
Suenan campanas de gloria
que dejan desierta la Universidad
Y allá en el templo del Apóstol Santo
con el estudiante hoy se va a casar
la galleguilla melosa, melosa
que oyendo esta copla ya no llorará
la galleguilla melosa, melosa
que oyendo esta copla ya no llorará

Local gastronomy

Galicia is, without a doubt, a paradise for food-lovers. Santiago's cuisine is typical of the region in that it is based on a wide variety of high-quality, fresh produce and traditional, healthy and tasty recipes.

The fame of Galician **fish and seafood** is well deserved, with a vast array of options on offer. Fish specialities served in the city's restaurants include hake, sea bass, sole, angler, grouper and turbot, either grilled or prepared Galician-style, while typical shellfish include scallops – strongly linked to the city because of the shape of their shell – oysters, clams, barnacles, spider crabs, lobster, crayfish and mussels.

The delicious **pulpo a feira** (octopus) is one of the highlights of Santiago's cuisine. Gallician meat also enjoys an enviable reputation, with numerous restaurants serving high-quality meat dishes. Typical regional specialities include the popular **empanada,** a delicious pie or pasty which comes with a vast array of fillings, including both meat and fish.

Grelos (turnip tops) are typical Gallician vegetables found in many traditional winter dishes, such as *lacón con grelos* (shoulder of pork, turnip tops, potatoes and chorizo), soup and Galician stew.

Visitors with a sweet tooth will want to taste the delicious **tarta de Santiago** (almond tart) and the tempting **filloas**, a type of sweet pancake.

J. Fiuza/MICHELIN

Delicious barnacles

J. Fiuza/MICHELIN

The famous Tarta de Santiago

Tarta de Santiago

Ingredients

Pastry: 1 egg, 125g/5oz sugar, two cups of flour, a pinch of cinnamon and a spoonful of water.

Filling: 4 eggs, 250g/10oz ground almonds, grated lemon rind, a pinch of cinnamon and icing sugar.

Preparation

To make the pastry, beat the egg with the water, sugar and cinnamon and gradually add the flour until the pastry reaches a consistency that can be worked with the hands. Roll the pastry out thinly and place in a pie dish greased with butter.

For the filling, whisk the eggs with the sugar and grated lemon peel and add the ground almonds and cinnamon. Fill the pastry dish with the mixture and place in a pre-heated oven at a temperature of 180°C/Gas Mark 4 for 30 minutes.

Once the tart is cooked, dust with icing sugar. If you want your tart to resemble those sold in local shops, cut a Santiago cross out of card and place it in the centre of the tart before dusting with icing sugar.

In terms of **wine**, Galicia currently has four quality-controlled areas *(denominaciones de origen)*: Rías Baixas, Ribeiro, Valdeorras and Ribeira Sacra y Monterrei.

The region's excellent local **brandies** or traditional **queimadas** (a hot drink made with grape liqueur, sugar and lemon) are a splendid way of rounding off a good dinner!

Handicrafts and souvenirs

A wide variety of interesting handicrafts and souvenirs are on sale in Santiago's shops. These include objects made from jet or silver, the two most typical materials used in the region, and other high-quality objects such as ceramics from Sargadelos or Galician fashion.

Silver and Jet

The names of two of the squares around the cathedral of Santiago, plaza de Azabachería and plaza de Platerías, recall the silver and jet industries which were already of major importance to the city in the Middle Ages – pilgrims travelling to Santiago often purchased jet or silver items to take home with them as a memento of their trip. Both of these trades have survived, thanks to the craftsmen who have passed on their skills from one generation to the next. Today most of these craftsmen, who until recently were based in the old town, have moved their workshops to other parts of the city; souvenir shops selling silver and jet and jewellery have opened in their place. Both silver and jet (hard black crystallised coal) are used to make a vast array of objects, many of which are related to the city's traditions, such as shells, crosses, pictures of the Apostle and incense burners, although necklaces, bracelets and pendants are increasingly being produced.

Sargadelos ceramics

The origins of Sargadelos ceramics date back to the early 19C when deposits of kaolin were discovered near the town and a factory was established here. Nowadays this ceramic work is one of the main symbols of Galician identity and an important part of any visit to the region. The historic centre of the town is full of souvenir shops, all of which sell these attractive ceramics dominated by the colours blue and white.

Galician fashion

Galicia plays an important role in the Spanish fashion world, with prestigious designers such as Adolfo Domínguez, Antonio Pernas, Roberto Verino and Kina Fernández all hailing from the region. Galicia is also home to Zara, the textile empire founded by Amancio Ortega.

H. González/MICHELIN

Ceramic plate of Sargadelos

Highlights

Cathedral★★★

The original church was built at the beginning of the 9C by the bishop Teodomiro over the Apostle's tomb shortly after its discovery. At the end of the same century, Alfonso III ordered the construction of a monastery and temple on the site of this new church; these were subsequently destroyed during the invasion by Al-Mansur. The cathedral visible today was built between the 11C-13C, although from the outside it looks more like a Baroque building.

Fachada del Obradoiro★★★

This Baroque masterpiece (its name means "work of gold") by **Fernando Casas y Novoa** has embellished the cathedral entrance since 1750. It is comprised of three richly sculptured sections each rising in triangular formation. The elegant twin towers standing majestically behind the two side sections are in perfect harmony with the ascendency of the façade, on which the interplay of straight and curved lines creates magnificent effects of both light and shade.

Pórtico de la Gloria★★★

The Doorway of Glory stands in the narthex, behind the Baroque façade. This magnificent Romanesque entrance shows great harmony in its expression and detail, marvellously

J. Fiuza/MICHELIN

Pórtico de la Gloria

J. Fiuza/MICHELIN   **Puerta de las Platerías**

depicted by over two hundred figures of exceptional beauty. Slightly more recent than the rest of the Romanesque cathedral, this masterpiece was the work of **Maestro Mateo** in the late 12C, hence its early-Gothic characteristics. Maestro Mateo strengthened the crypt below the doorway in order for it to support its weight. The central portal is dedicated to the Christian Church: the tympanum shows the Saviour surrounded by the four Evangelists, while the 24 Elders of the Apocalypse are depicted on the archivolt in a sedentary position. The engaged pillars are covered in statues of Apostles and Prophets. Note the figure of Daniel with the hint of a smile, a precursor to the famous Smiling Angel in Reims Cathedral in France. The pillar beneath the seated figure of St James bears finger marks upon the stone; traditionally, on entering the cathedral, exhausted pilgrims placed their hands here in token of safe arrival. On the other side of the pillar, the statue known as the "saint of bumps" is believed to impart memory and wisdom to whoever bumps his forehead against it.

The side doors are devoted to purgatory or the Synagogue (to the left) and to hell or the Heathen (to the right).

Interior

☎ *981 56 05 27.* The immense Romanesque cathedral into which pilgrims crowded in the Middle Ages has remained intact with all the characteristics of pilgrim churches at the time: a Latin cross floor plan, vast proportions, an ambulatory and a triforium.

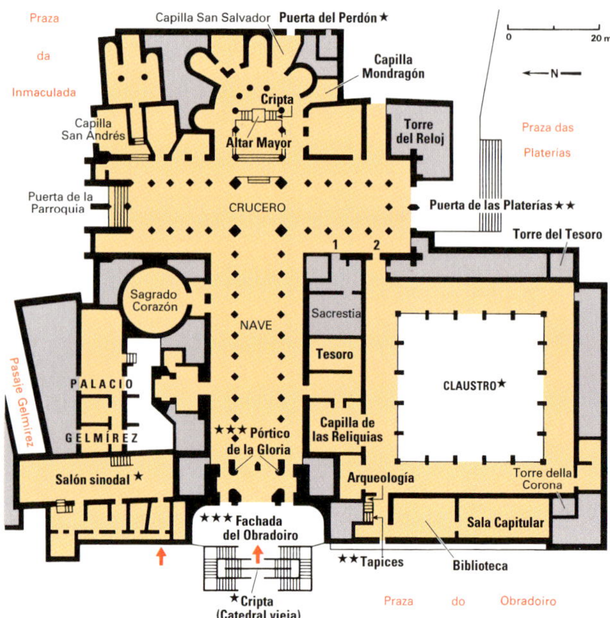

The nave and transept, complete with aisles, are plain yet majestic, aesthetic yet functional. The triforium rises above the side aisles supported by a barrel vault, providing direct illumination for the central nave through twin bays. The side aisles are covered with 13C groin vaults. At major festivals a huge incense burner, the **botafumeiro** *(displayed in the library)*, is hung from the transept dome keystone and swung to the eaves by eight men pulling on a rope.

The decoration in the sanctuary is surprisingly exuberant for a Romanesque setting. The **altar mayor** or high altar, surmounted by a sumptuously apparelled 13C statue of St James, is covered by a gigantic baldaquin (pilgrims mounting the stairs behind the altar may kiss the saint's mantle). Beneath the altar is the **crypt**, built into the foundations of the 9C church which contained St James' tomb, and now containing the relics of the saint and his two disciples, St Theodore and St Athanasius. Particularly beautiful among the cathedral's many outstanding features is the Gothic vaulting of the Capilla Mondragón (1521), and the 9C Capilla de la Corticela, which at the time of its construction was separate from the cathedral.

The Renaissance doors to the **sacristía** (sacristy) *(1)* and *claustro* (cloisters) *(2)* on the right arm of the transept are also worthy of note.

VISITS OF THE CATHEDRAL ROOF
A tour of the roof provides a different and unusual perspective of Santiago's cathedral, as well as some memorable views of the city's skyline. Not to be missed!
Entrance through Palacio Gelmírez. Guided tours: 1hr. ☎ 981 55 29 85.

Museum

☎ 981 56 05 27. The museum consists of three distinct parts. Access to the **tesoro** (treasury), occupying a Gothic chapel to the right of the nave, is via the inside of the cathedral. Exhibits on display include a gold and silver monstrance by Antonio de Arfe (1539-66). The entrance to the **crypt★**, built in the 11C to compensate for differences in floor level and to support the Pórtico de la Gloria, is via the Plaza del Obradoiro; this entrance is partially obscured by the large staircase beneath the Obradoiro façade. This is in fact a small Romanesque church with a Latin cross plan and attractive columns and sculpted capitals. Access to the rooms devoted to

J. Fiuza/MICHELIN

Puerta Santa

the cathedral's archaeological excavations, the **biblioteca** (library), where the *botafumeiros* are displayed, the **sala capitular** (chapter house) with its impressive granite vault and walls hung with 16C Flemish tapestries, and the balcony rooms, displaying **tapestries**★★ by Goya, Bayeu, Rubens and Teniers, is through a side entrance.

Cloisters★

These Renaissance cloisters were designed by Juan de Álava who, in line with architectural trends at the beginning of the 16C, combined a Gothic structure with Plateresque decoration. The cloisters were completed by Rodrigo Gil de Hontañón and Gaspar de Arce.

J. Fiuza/MICHELIN

Puerta de las Platerías★★

The Silversmiths' Doorway is the only 12C Romanesque doorway to have been preserved. Not all of the entrance we see today is original, as many of the sculptures were taken from the Puerta de la Azabachería. The most impressive figure is without doubt that of David playing the viola on the left door. Adam and Eve can be seen being driven out of the Garden of Eden; the Pardoning of the Adulterous Woman is also distinguishable on the right-hand corner of the left tympanum. The **Torre del Reloj** (Clock Tower), on the right, was added at the end of the 17C. To the left, stands the **Torre del Tesoro** (Treasury Tower).

Plaza de la Quintana

Exploring the city

From plaza del Obradoiro to plaza de la Quintana★★

This itinerary begins in the delightful plaza del Obradoiro. The magnificent buildings surrounding the square provide a spectacular backdrop for one of the city's architectural highlights.

Palacio Gelmírez (Pazo Xelmírez)

☎ 981 57 23 00. The bishops' palace stands to the left of the cathedral. Some 12C and Gothic-style apartments are open to the public, including the vast **Salón Sinodal★** (Synod Hall), which is more than 30m/98ft long and has sculptured ogive vaulting. Carved in high relief on the bosses are scenes from the wedding banquet of Alfonso IX de León.

Hostal de los Reyes Católicos★

The hostelry, founded by Ferdinand of Aragón and Isabel of Castilla as a pilgrim inn and hospital and now a parador,

J. Fiuza/MICHELIN

has an impressive **façade★** with a splendid Plateresque doorway. The hospital's plan of a cross within a square, which creates four elegant Plateresque patios, was common to hospitals of the period.

Ayuntamiento

Opposite the cathedral is the severely Classical 18C façade of the former **Pazo de Raxoi**, a palace designed by the French architect Charles Lemaur. Today, the building serves as the town hall and the headquarters of the regional government, the Xunta de Galicia.

Colegio de San Jerónimo (San Xerome)

The college, a 17C building on the square's south side, has an elegant 15C gateway with a strong Romanesque influence.

Iglesia de San Fructuoso

This church, also known as the Iglesia de las Angustias, was built in the 18C in Churrigueresque style, with a façade designed to be seen from plaza del Obradoiro; because the square stands at a higher elevation, the most interesting aspects of the church's abundant decoration can be

Pazo de Raxoi

seen on its upper section. Note the large coat of arms of Spain, the broken cornice – above which stand the images of the four cardinal virtues – and the bell tower. A statue of the Virgen de las Angustias (Virgin of Anguish) is housed in a niche above the entrance doorway. The main feature of interest inside the church is the cupola crowning the transept.

Rúa do Franco

This busy street is lined by old colleges, such as the Colegio de Fonseca, numerous shops and typical bars.

Colegio de Fonseca – Archbishop Alonso de Fonseca ordered the construction of this impressive Renaissance-style college in the 16C to house the recently established Universidad Compostelana. The façade comprises two floors embellished with columns and Gothic statues, which also frame the window of the upper floor. The coat of arms of the Fonseca family, featuring five stars, can be seen in the centre, above the main door. The attractive patio stands at the heart of the building. Other features of note are the hall (to the left of the entrance), with its magnificent Mudéjar *artesonado* ceiling, and the chapel (to the right of the entrance). Today, the college is home to the university's main library.

Before reaching the porta da Faxeiras, turn left towards plaza do Toural.

Plaza do Toural is fronted by the **Pazo de Bendaña**, an 18C palace whose façade

J. Fiuza/MICHELIN

bears the coat of arms of the Bendaña family supporting a globe. Nowadays the building is home to the Fundación Eugenio Granell *(see "Museums")*.

Nearby, on the corner of rúa do Vilar and the callejón de Entrerrúas, the narrowest street in the city, note the 18C **Casa-Pazo de Vaamonde**, a large arcaded house adorned with a coat of arms.

Head along callejón de Entrerrúas as far as rúa Nova.

Rúa Nova

This busy shopping street running parallel to rúa Franco and rúa do Vilar is flanked by a number of old town houses.

Antiguo Colegio dos Irlandeses – Pazo Ramirás – As a result of the persecution suffered by Catholics in Ireland in the 16C, colleges were establised to train the Irish clergy in several European countries. One of these was built in Santiago, although the building visible today was erected in the 18C over the ruins of the former college.

Iglesia de Santa María Salomé – With the exception of the doorway, virtually nothing remains of the original church built on the site in the 12C during the time of Archbishop Gelmírez. The prominent portico dates from the 15C, the sculptures adorning the façade the 14C and 15C, and the Baroque bell tower the 18C. Several Baroque sculptures from the Compostela School are on display inside.

Casa-Pazo dos Fonseca – *At the back of Iglesia de Santa María Salomé*. The lower sec-

Colegio de Fonseca

tion with four round arches supported on columns is all that remains of the original 16C palace; the walls were enclosed at a later date. The pendentives of the arches are decorated with medallions. Note also the escutcheons (supported by tritons) on the corners.

The **Iglesia and Colegio das Orfas** are located nearby, in the street of the same name. Built in the 17C, the college was founded to harbour girl orphans; nowadays it is home to the Nuestra Señora de los Remedios school.

Return to rúa Nova, passing in front of the **Teatro Principal**, dating from 1842.

Casa das Pomas – This late-17C porticoed house is striking for the pilasters, consisting of a series of fruits hanging from a shell, which frame the two upper floors.

Pazo de Santa Cruz – Built in the early 19C, this attractive small palace has three floors adorned with iron balconies. The central section of the façade is crowned by a pediment bearing the coat of arms of the Marqués de Santa Cruz.

Turn left along calle de Xelmírez and continue to rúa do Vilar.

Rúa do Vilar

The street is bordered by old arcaded houses.

Casa do Deán – This three-storey palatial mansion on the corner of calle Xelmirez dates from the mid-18C. The decoration, which is con-

centrated around the main door, consists of a series of volutes, pinnacles and attributes relating to St James. Note also the projecting balcony above the door. Today, the Casa do Dean is home to the Pilgrims' Office (Oficina del Peregrino).

Casa del Cabildo

The attractive front of this unusual building stands opposite the Puerta de Platerías, the appearance of which it almost replicates, and the Fuente de los Caballos. The façade, adorned with fine Baroque decoration, has a depth of more than 3m/10ft and was built to enclose and embellish the plaza de Platerías.

Plaza de la Quintana★★

This famous square, always busy with students, stands at the east end of the cathedral by the **Puerta del Perdón★** (Door of Pardon) or **Puerta Santa** (Holy Door), built by Fernández Lechuga in 1611. The door, which is only opened in Holy Years, incorporates all the statues of the Prophets and Patriarchs carved by Maestro Mateo for the original Romanesque choir.

The square is enclosed by a number of interesting buildings.

Casa da Conga – The Casa da Conga (Canonical House) fronts the south side of the square. Erected at the beginning of the 18C, it is a large building with arcades formed by rounded arches resting on columns.

Casa de la Parra – This impressive late-17C Baroque edifice stands opposite the Casa da Conga at the top of a flight of steps. On the façade, note the carved bunches of grapes on either side of the doors, as well as the corbels that support the unbroken balcony on the first floor. Nowadays, the building is used as an exhibition hall.

Monasterio de San Paio de Antealtares – The building standing today dates from the 17C and 18C, although the monastery was originally founded in the 9C, when Alfonso II the Chaste decreed that a monastery should be erected to house the recently discovered sepulchre of St James the Apostle. The long wall running along the east side of the plaza de Quintana is sober in style, its monotony broken only by windows decorated with wrought-iron grilles. The building now houses the **Museo de Arte Sacro** (see "Museums").

Praza do Toural

From plaza de la Universidad to plaza de Cervantes

The bustling plaza de la Universidad and plaza de Mazarelos are fronted by several interesting buildings.

University

The university stands on the site originally occupied by the Colegio de la Compañía and is now home to the Faculty of Geography and History. Built in the 18C, it is neo-Classical in design, with a portal comprising four gigantic Ionic columns and the four statues of the institution's benefactors. The building is centred around large cloisters.

Former Iglesia de la Compañía

This 17C church, now used as an exhibition hall, is located next to the Faculty of Geography and History. Following the expulsion of the Jesuits from Spain at the end of the 18C it became the university chapel. At the time, the statues on the façade represent-

J. Fiuza/MICHELIN

ing St Ignatius and St Francis were transformed into images of St Peter and St Paul. An interesting Baroque altarpiece is displayed inside.

Pass through the **Arco de Mazarelos**, the only gateway that has been preserved from the old city walls.

Convento and Iglesia de las Madres Mercedarias

Located outside the old city walls, this imposing 17C convent stands opposite the Arco de Mazarelos. The façade of the convent church is neo-Classical in style.

Convento del Colegio da Compañía de María or Convento da Ensinanza

Founded in the 17C, this sober, large-proportioned building was established as a school for the girls from the noble classes. Note the archiepiscopal escutcheon on the pediment of the church façade.

From here, head along the impressive rúa das Trompas as far as the Convento de Belvís.

Convento de Belvís

This convent stands on a hill on the outskirts of the city. The building visible today dates from the beginning of the 18C, although the convent was originally founded in the 14C. The Virgin of the Portico (Virgen del Portal) is venerated inside this 18C church, designed by Fernando Casas y Novoa.

Retrace your steps to reach plaza de San Fiz de Solivio.

Iglesia de San Fiz de Solovio

According to tradition, this church is the oldest in Santiago, since it was on this

Façade detail of the university

J. Fiuza/MICHELIN

Tympanum, Iglesia de San Fiz

spot that the hermit Pelayo, who discovered the remains of the Apostle, lived. A chapel was later built on the site (this was subsequently destroyed by Al-Mansor), followed by a Romanesque church in the 12C – only the doorway with its distinctive horseshoe arches remains from this building. A 14C depiction of the Adoration of the Magi is represented on the tympanum. The existing church and tower both date from the 18C.

Head to the Pazo de Feijoo.

Pazo de Feijoo

This 18C palace-mansion was designed by Domingo de Andrade. Note the large iron balcony on the first floor and the coats of arms on the floor above it.

Return to the Iglesia de San Fiz and take calle das Ameas. This street is home to a busy **mar-** **ket**, which is well worth a visit.

Convento and Iglesia de San Agustín (Santo Agostiño)

This 17C convent and church fronts the square of the same name. On the neo-Classical façade, note the statue of the Virgin above the door, in addition to the coat of arms of Spain on the upper section. Originally the façade had two towers, although only one remains. The convent now belongs to the Jesuits and houses a university hall of residence.

Turn into rúa Travesa.

Iglesia de Santa María del Camino

This Romanesque church, rebuilt in the 18C, stands close to the Porta do Camiño, through which pilgrims on the French Way would enter the

city. The façade, crowned by a bell tower, is adorned with two pairs of massive Ionic pilasters and a curved pediment. The main features of interest inside the church are the neo-Classical Immaculate Conception, the main altarpiece and a Gothic relief of the Epiphany.
Turn left along Casas Reais.

Palacio de Fondevila

The outstanding feature of this palace built in the typical Compostela Baroque style in the mid-17C is the large escutcheon adorning the chamfer. Note also the characteristic projecting balconies.

Iglesia das Ánimas

This neo-Classical church on the opposite side of the street dates from the 18C.

Of particular note on the façade, embellished with Ionic columns and a pediment, is the relief depicting souls *(ánimas)* in purgatory above the door, and two angels and a cross on the upper section. On the reception floor inside, the reliefs of the Passion and the Resurrection are particularly impressive.

Iglesia de San Benito del Campo

Plaza de Cervantes, formally known as the plaza de San Benito, is home to this small church built in neo-Classical style above an earlier edifice erected during the medieval period. A number of fine Baroque sculptures are on display inside the church.

J. Fiuza/MICHELIN

Palacio de Fondevila

From plaza de Cervantes to plaza del Obradoiro

Casa-Museo da Troia

Rúa da Troia, 5. ☎ 981 59 51 59. This typical 18C house in the old quarter was used in the late 19C as a student hostal; it was immortalised by the writer Alejandro Pérez Lugín in his novel *La Casa de la Troya*. Nowadays, the building houses a museum recreating the atmosphere of the hostal during this period.

Exit onto plaza de San Martín.

Monasterio de San Martín Pinario★

☎ *981 58 30 08.* The monastery church overlooking plaza San Martín, preceded by a double flight of stairs, has an ornate **façade**, similar in style to a Plateresque altarpiece. The interior consists of a surprisingly wide single aisle covered by coffered barrel vaulting. It is lit by a Byzantine-style lantern without a drum. The high altar **retable★**, in the most ornate Churrigueresque manner, is by the great architect Casa y Novoa (1730). On either side are Baroque pulpits canopied by cottage-loaf-shaped sounding boards. A grand staircase beneath an elegant cupola leads to three 16C-18C cloisters, one of which is the Claustro de las Procesiones (Processions Cloister).

The monastery façade overlooking plaza de la Inmaculada is colossal in style with massive Doric columns in pairs rising from the ground to the roof. Plaza de la Azabachería opposite is so named because of the guild of jet craftsmen (*azabacheros*) who had their workshops in this square.

Return to plaza de San Martín and head along rúa San Miguel.

Iglesia de San Miguel Dos Agros

The sober façade of this 17C neo-Classical church is decorated with two pairs of fluted pilasters supporting a pediment.

The **Casa Gótica**, opposite, is home to the Museo de las Peregrinaciones (*see "Museums"*).

Pazo de Amarante

In rúa de Algalia de Abaixo. This small palace is crowned by a pediment bearing the coat of arms of the Amarante-Camarasa family who ordered its construction in the 18C.

Cross rúa das Rodas and turn into rúa San Roque.

Antiguo Hospital and Iglesia de San Roque

Built in the 16C and remodeled two centuries later,

Monasterio de San Martín Pinario

this former hospital has preserved its simple façade, including the escutcheon of its founding archbishop above the door. The Baroque-style church contains an 18C altarpiece by Simón Rodríguez.

Convento de Santa Clara

Although the convent was founded in the 13C, the present building dates from the late 17C and early 18C. Note the unusual curtain façade, Baroque in style, which leads to the garden. The decoration is concentrated on the central section and on the upper part of the building, which is crowned by several large cylindrical features. An early-18C altarpiece by Domingo Andrade adorns the inside of the church.

Convento del Carmen (Convento do Carme)

This convent for discalced Carmelite nuns was erected in the 18C. The simple façade, crowned by the Virgin of the Carmelites (Virgen del Carmen), is in perfect harmony with the characteristic austerity of this order.

Return to rúa das Rodas, then follow Costa Vella.

Convento de San Francisco

It is said that St Francis of Assisi founded this convent in 1214, when he undertook a pilgrimage to Santiago. Legend relates that the saint entrusted its construction to a charcoal-maker named Cotolay, who miraculously discovered treasure that enabled him to finance the project. Of the original convent, built in Gothic style, just five arches in the cloisters have been preserved. The present Baroque church was erected in the 17C.

The convent now houses the **Museo de Terra Santa** (see "Museums").

A large **cross**, a work by Asorey, was erected in front of the convent in 1930 and narrates scenes from the life of St Francis.

Faculdad de Medicina

The imposing Faculty of Medicine fronts calle San Francisco, next to the side façade of the Parador de los Reyes Católicos. This building, with its classic lines, dates from the early 20C.

. Fiuza/MICHELIN

Santa Clara convent

Museums and sights of interest

Colegiata de Santa María del Sar

Museums

Museo do Pobo Galego

☎ *981 58 36 20, www.museo dopobo.es.* The Museum of the Galician People is housed in the former **Convento de San Domingos de Bonaval**, founded in the 13C. Of the original building, only the 13C-14C church has been preserved, although it has undergone subsequent modification. The church, which has the unique feature of being the only surviving example of the mendicant Gothic style in the city, houses the **Panteón de Gallegos Ilustres** (Pantheon of Illustrious Galicians), including Castelao, Rosalía de Castro etc.

The present convent, a reconstruction and expansion of the original building, was erected in the 17C and 18C and is a work by Domingo Andrade. The triple **spiral staircase**★, with three independent ramps leading to the different floors, is of particular interest, and is considered one of the most exceptional examples of architecture in the city.

The **museum** provides a general insight into the major aspects that define Galician culture: the **sea** (boats, fishing methods, models etc), **traditional trades**, the **countryside** (working tools, weights and measures, models etc), **costumes** (traditional working and festive garments and knitted lace), **music** (traditional instruments, ranging from the

J. Fiuza/MICHELIN

Museo do Pobo Galego

J. Fiuza/MICHELIN   **Centro Galego de Arte Contemporánea**

famous bagpipes to the *chirimía* – a type of oboe), **stone and metalwork** (jet, marble, gold, silver and tin) and **habitat** (different types of houses, ancillary buildings and structures such as barns, windmills, ovens etc). The museum also includes sections on **archaeology** (in the cloisters), **paintings** (16C to the early 20C) and **sculpture** (contemporary).

Centro Galego de Arte Contemporánea

☎ 981 54 66 19. www.cgac.org. The magnificent centre for contemporary Galician art, designed by the leading Portuguese architect Alvaro Siza, was built between 1988 and 1993 on land formerly occupied by the vegetable garden of the Convento de San Domingos de Bonaval. Racionalist in concept, the building's design is based on the interplay of different volumes, light and expansive surfaces. The stunning views from the terrace on the top floor encompass the city's historical quarter.

The aim of the centre is to introduce contemporary art to a wider audience through a full and varied programme that includes retrospectives by artists with an international reputation, exhibitions by leading contemporary Galician artists, and specific projects created for the centre by young Galician, Spanish and foreign artists.

Museo das Peregrinacións (de las Peregrinaciones)

☎ *981 58 15 58. www.mdper egrinacions.com.* The Pilgrimage Museum occupies the building known as the Casa Gótica, a 14C house to which additional sections were added three centuries later. It was long thought that this medieval construction was the residence of King Pedro I the Cruel, although there is no firm proof of this.

The small museum is dedicated to the origins and history of the pilgrimage to Santiago through engravings, models, gold and silverwork, statues, ornaments etc. The museum highlights the pilgrimage's importance as a religious phenomenon and its influence on the birth and development of the city in parallel with the worship of the Apostle, while at the same time displaying iconography depicting St James as an apostle, pilgrim and "slayer of the Moors" *(matamoros)*. The rituals and customs associated with the Way of St James are also highlighted.

Museo de Arte Sacra

981 58 31 27. The Monasterio de San Paio de Antealtares is home to the city's Museum of Sacred Art, with its interesting collection of sculptures, paintings, gold and silverwork, and liturgical ornaments and documents. Exhibits worthy of particular note include the Apostle's original altar, a magnificent 13C Christ, which belonged to the monastery, a silver reliquary with the arm of St Pelayo, and an edition of

the Rules of St Benedict, dating from 1610.

Museo de Terra Santa

☏ *981 58 16 00. Closed for restoration.* This museum, housed in one of the cloisters of the Monasterio de San Francisco, is entirely devoted to the Holy Land, along with Rome, the other main Christian pilgrimage centre. Displays include models of several historic buildings in Jerusalem, a collection of coins (from the time of Alexander the Great to the modern day), as well as traditional objects from the area.

Fundación Eugenio Granell

☏ *981 57 63 94. www.fundacion-granell.org.* The Palacio de Bendaña is the headquarters of this foundation which takes its name from the surrealist artist Eugenio Granell (b La Coruña 1912 – d Madrid 2001). The foundation's collection is based on the extensive portfolio of this artist, a number of Afro-Cuban works of art, and exhibits donated by the English surrealist artist Philip West. The aim of the foundation is to promote the work of Granell, surrealism and other related artistic trends to a wider audience. The three rooms on the first floor are used to display the foundation's collection on a rotating basis. The second floor is devoted to temporary exhibitions.

Convento de San Francisco

Other places of interest

Parque de la Alameda

Santiago's most famous park is the perfect place to stroll and relax after spending time exploring the city. The Baroque **Iglesia de O Pilar** (alongside avenida Xoan Carlos I), a late-19C bandstand, and the **Iglesia de Santa Susana** are all located within the boundaries of the park. The latter, crowning a wooded hill, was founded by Archbishop Gelmírez in the 12C. With the exception of the doorway, virtually nothing remains of the original Romanesque structure. The church visible today was rebuilt in the 17C and 18C.

Colegio de San Clemente

This college, also known as the Colegio de Pasantes, dates from the 17C. Its main features of interest are the chapel and the central patio. Today it houses the Instituto Rosalía de Castro.

Colegiata de Santa María del Sar*

☎ *981 56 28 91.* This 12C Romanesque collegiate church has an unusual external appearance brought about by the addition of buttresses in the 18C. The necessity of these becomes apparent when you enter the church, given the astonishing

J. Fiuza/MICHELIN   **Parque de la Alameda**

J. Fiuza/MICHELIN

Colegiata de Santa María del Sar

slant of the pillars caused by the pressure of the vaulting. The only remaining Romanesque cloisters, standing next to the church, are attributed to Maestro Mateo or his school, and comprise elegant paired **arches*** and capitals decorated with floral motifs.

The small museum displays items of 18C gold and silverwork from the city's workshops, historical documents (including a parchment dating from 1136 relating to the founding of the church), and exhibits taken from the Romanesque cloisters.

Pazo de San Lourenzo de Trasouto

The original manor dates from the 13C although little remains from this period apart from a few arches on the church portico. Most of the building visible today is the result of construction work carried out in the 17C and 18C. The highlight of the church interior is undoubtedly the magnificent 16C Renaissance altarpiece carved from Carrara marble, brought here from the Convento de San Francisco in Sevilla by the Counts of Altamira, who owned the building in the 19C.

Auditorio de Galicia

This modern granite auditorium, crowned by a copper roof, was designed by Julio Cano Lasso and Diego Cano Pintos and opened in 1989. It is pleasantly situated next to a small lake in the Parque da Música.

Monasterio and Iglesia de Santa María de Conxo

This monastery was founded in the 12C in the Conxo district of the city, although the wings of the cloisters are the only sections that remain from this period. The present building, Baroque in style, dates from the 17C. Inside the church, note the splendid altarpiece adorned with magnificent statues, in particular a Christ by Gregorio Fernández.

Places of interest around Santiago

Pazo de Oca*

Around 25km/15.5mi SE along the N 525. On the way to this famous Galician manor house it is worth stopping at the **Pico Sacro** *(turn left in Lestedo)* to enjoy the delightful views across the Ulla valley, with Santiago in the distance. A small Romanesque chapel stands on top of the hill.

Return to the main road. A little further on, on the right, you pass the **Pazo de Santa Cruz de Ribadulla**, with its attractive gardens.

Pazo de Oca – ☎ 986 58 74 35. This austere Galician **manor**, or *pazo*, with

B. Brillion/MICHELIN

a crenellated tower, lines two sides of a vast square adorned with a cross. The romantic **park**✶✶ behind the manor comes as a complete surprise, with its terraces and lakes, shady arbours and intimate corners.

Ponte Maceira

Around 20km/12mi NW. Take the C 543, turning right in Bertamiráns. Time appears to have stood still in this picturesque small village in a delightful setting on the banks of the River Tambre. The main attractions here are the medieval bridge spanning the river, the old water mills and the charm of Ponte Maceira's traditional Galician architecture.

The bridge links Ponte Maceira with **Negreira**, where the main building of interest is the impressive Pazo de Cotón.

Padrón

20km/12mi S along the N 550. See "Excursions" Rías Bajas.

Pazo de Oca

Excursions

A Coruña / La Coruña★

Population: 252 694. Michelin map 571 B 4 – Michelin La Coruña city plan 19082. The economic capital of the Comunidad Gallega is located 73km/ 45.5mi N of Santiago de Compostela along the AP 9 motorway. ▣ Dársena de la Marina, 15001 A Coruña, ☎ 981 22 18 22.

This pleasant Galician city stands on a rocky islet, linked to the mainland by a narrow strip of sand. The lighthouse stands to the north, the curved harbour to the south, along with the impressive glass tower of the pleasure port, while the west side of the isthmus is dominated by the sandy Riazor and Orzán beaches.

Three distinct quarters testify to La Coruña's growth: the **City** (Ciudad), at the northern end of the harbour, a charming old quarter with its small peaceful squares and Romanesque churches; the business and commercial centre on the isthmus, with its wide avenues and shopping streets (**avenida de Los Cantones, calle Real** and **calle San Andrés**); and, to the south, the **Ensanche**, home to warehouses and industrial premises, a reminder that La Coruña is the sixth largest commercial port in Spain as well as an important industrial and fishing centre.

A stroll through the Old Town

The old town *(ciudad vieja)* occupies the original settlement at the northern end of the harbour. This quarter is characterised by narrow cobbled streets and peaceful squares.

Colegiata de Santa María del Campo – This Romanesque church has three barrel-vaulted naves strengthened by arches with plaster

---

THE INVINCIBLE ARMADA

It was from La Coruña that Philip II's **Armada** set sail in 1588. The fleet of 130 men-of-war, manned by 10 000 sailors and transporting 19 000 soldiers, set out for England ostensibly to punish Elizabeth for the execution of Mary, Queen of Scots, and with a final aim of preventing further attacks on Spanish ships by pirates, and putting an end to the support that the Queen of England was providing rebels from the Low Countries. Poor weather forced the Armada to take refuge in the port of La Coruña until 22 July, giving the forewarned English time to prepare for battle. The ill-fated fleet was easily out-manœuvred by the English, and was ultimately destroyed in another storm off the coast of Flanders, when deprived of ports offering shelter. Upon hearing of the disaster, which saw the loss of 63 ships and 15 000 men, Philip II exclaimed: "Send more men to fight against men, not the elements". The defeat marked the end of Spanish naval power, and marked the beginning of the end for its Empire.

A year later, in 1589, Elizabeth sent Sir Francis Drake to attack the Iberian coast. La Coruña was saved by **María Pita**, who seized the English flag from the standard-bearer as the invaders were scaling the walls of the city, and raised the alarm.

Torre de Hércules

A CORUÑA

Cantón Grande	AZ	7
Cantón Pequeño	AZ	8
Compostela	AZ	13
Damas	BY	14
Ferrol	AZ	18
Finisterre (Av. de)	AZ	19
Gómez Zamalloa	AZ	20
Herrerías	BY	23
Juan Canalejo	AY	25
Juana de Vega (Av.)	AZ	26
Maestranza	BY	27
María Pita (Pl. de)	BY	28
Padre Feijóo	AZ	32
Payo Gómez	AZ	36
Picavia	AZ	37
Pontevedra (Pl. de)	AZ	40
Real	AY	
Riego del Agua	BY	42
Rubine (Av. de)	AZ	45
San Agustín	BY	46
San Agustín (Cuesta de)	BY	47
San Andrés	AYZ	
Sánchez Bregua	AZ	50
Santa Catalina	AZ	52
Santa María	BY	51
Teresa Herrera	AZ	55

Colegiata de Santa María del Campo	BY	M¹
Museo de Bellas Artes	AY	M²

borders. The fine 13C-14C portal, Gothic rose window and the tower are worthy of particular interest on the exterior. A **Museum of Sacred Art** (Museo de Arte Sacro) is housed on one side of the church.

Note the attractive 15C Calvary in the square between Santa María and an impressive Baroque house.

Plazuela de Santa Bárbara – This peaceful square, which hosts chamber music concerts during August (Fiestas de María Pita), lies in the protective shadow of Santa Bárbara convent's high, sombre walls. Above the doorway of the convent is a Romanesque lintel depicting the weighing of souls in the presence of Christ.

Jardín de San Carlos – It is in this attractive park that General John Moore, who was killed in the Battle of Elviña, is buried.

Castillo de San Antón: Museo Arqueológico e Histórico – This fortress, which dates from the period of Philip II, formed part of La Coruña's system of defence in former times (*see description under "Worth a Visit"*).

Iglesia de Santiago – The church's north door and three apses, overlooking plaza de Azcárraga, are Romanesque. The west door – showing the figures of St John and St Mark carved against the piers – and the massive arches supporting the timber roof above the nave, are Gothic. The church contains a beautifully carved stone pulpit.

El Centro

The city's central district acts as a natural extension to the old quarter. Nowadays it is a lively commercial area.

Avenida de la Marina★ – The avenue, facing the harbour, is lined by tall houses with glassed-in balconies typical of La Coruña. Extending it on one side is the paseo de la Dársena and on the other the attractively landscaped **Jardines de Méndez Núñez**, gardens with a variety of flowering trees.

Plaza de María Pita – The vast pedestrian square just behind avenida de la Marina is named after the town's 16C heroine. It is fronted by the Ayuntamiento (City Hall), arcades, galleries and lively bar and restaurant terraces.

Worth a Visit

Castillo de San Antón: Museo Arqueológico e Histórico – ☎ 981 18 98 50. The castle's casemates served as a prison for several famous inmates such as Malaspina. It now houses an archaeological museum, which includes a room dedicated to prehistoric gold and silverware.

Museo de Bellas Artes – ☎ 981 22 37 23. The main feature of this modern fine arts museum is the light and spacious feel of its exhibition rooms, dedicated to art from the 16C to the 20C. Of particular note are the sketches by Goya.

Domus-Casa del Hombre – ☎ 981 18 98 40. This unusual **building★**, designed by the Japanese architect **Arata Isozaki**, is located on the Riazor bay, and has become one of the architectural symbols of the city. The façade, facing the bay, is composed of a double curve which adopts the shape of a large sail, and is covered with pieces of slate to give a scaly appearance. The building's other wall has made use of the city's old quarry to create an area of large stone blocks which act as a screen. The museum itself is dedicated to Man, and deals with various aspects of human life such as genetics, reproduction and the senses through texts, photographs, interactive displays, holographs etc.

Aquarium Finisterrae – ☎ 981 18 98 42. Also known as the Casa de los Peces (House of the Fish), the city's aquarium is located close to the Torre de Hércules. Its main role is to highlight to visitors the marine ecosystems in the waters off the Galician coast. Large tanks in the main exhibition room, the Maremagnum, display several of these ecosystems, including the continental shelf, banks of algae etc.

Torre de Hércules – ☏ 981 22 37 30. This tower was built in the 2C AD and is the oldest functioning lighthouse in the world. In 1790, when Charles III modified the tower to its present square shape, the original outer ramp was enclosed to form an inner staircase. From the top (104m/341ft), there is a **view** of the town and the coast.

C. Jaffres/MICHELIN

Around La Coruña

Cambre – *11km/7mi S.* ☎ *981 67 51 57.* The main attraction in this rustic small town is the 12C Romanesque **Iglesia de Santa María***, with a charming façade divided into three sections corresponding with the nave and two aisles inside. Multifoil arches – emphasising the windows on either side – and the buttress capitals show distinct Moorish influence. The tympanum is carved with the Holy Lamb in a medallion supported by angels. In the interior, with its great purity of style, note the apse circled by an **ambulatory** with five radiating chapels.

Plaza de María Pita

Lugo★

Population: 87 605. Michelin map 571 C 7. Lugo is situated approximately 120km/80mi from Santiago de Compostela along the AP 9 and A 6 motorways and 103km/64mi from the city via the N 547 and N 540 national roads. The town enjoys an impressive, elevated setting (485m/ 1 591ft) on the left bank of the River Miño. ⬧ Praza Maior 27, 27001 Lugo, ☎ 982 23 13 61.

What was once the capital of the province of Gallaecia under the Romans is now a pleasant town with wide shopping streets and squares (eg rúa da Raiña and plaza de Santo Domingo) and a distinguished old quarter huddled around the cathedral. The town's walls, old bridge and thermal baths still survive from Roman times.

Old Town

Muralla★★ – The walls were built by the Romans in the 3C, although they have undergone significant modifications since that time, particularly during the Middle Ages.

They are made of schist slabs levelled off at a uniform 10m/33ft to form a continuous perimeter over 2km/1.2mi long with 10 gateways into the old quarter. In 2000, the walls were declared a World Heritage Site by UNESCO.

Cathedral★ – The Romanesque church (1129) was modified in later years by Gothic and Baroque additions. The Chapel of the Wide-Eyed Virgin (Capilla de la Virgen de los Ojos Grandes), at the east end, by Fernando Casas y Novoa, has a Baroque rotunda enhanced by a stone balustrade. The north doorway, sheltered by a 15C porch, has a fine Romanesque **Christ in Majesty**★. The figure is above a capital curiously suspended in mid-air and carved with the Last Supper.

Inside, the Romanesque nave is roofed with barrel vaulting and lined with galleries, a feature common in pilgrimage churches. Two immense wooden Renaissance altarpieces stand at the ends of the transept – the one on the south side is signed by the sculptor Cornelis de Holanda (1531). A door in the west wall of the south transept leads to the small but elegant **cloisters**.

City squares – The 18C **Palacio Episcopal**, facing the

LUGO

Ánxel López Pérez (Av.)	Z	2
Bispo Aguirre	Z	3
Bolaño Rivadeneira	Y	5
Campo (Pr. do)	Z	8
Comandante Manso (Pr.)	Z	12
Conde Pallarés	Z	15
Coruña (Av. da)	Y	21
Cruz	Z	23
Dezaoito de Xullo (Av. do)	Y	24
Doctor Castro	Z	27
Marior (Pr.)	Z	30
Montero Ríos (Av.)	Z	37
Paxariños	Z	39
Pío XII (Pr. de)	Z	43
Progreso	Y	47
Quiroga Ballesteros	Y	50
Raíña	Y	53
Ramón Ferreiro	Z	56
Rodríguez Mourelo (Av.)	Z	62
San Fernando	Y	65
San Marcos	Y	68
San Pedro	Z	71
Santa María (Pr. de)	Z	74
Santo Domingo (Pr. de)	YZ	77
Teatro	Y	78
Teniente Coronel Teijeiro	YZ	79
Tinería	Z	80
Vilalba	Z	83

Ayuntamiento	Z	H
Catedral	Z	A
Museo Provincial	Y	M
Palacio episcopal	Z	B

north door of the cathedral on **plaza de Santa María**, is a typical *pazo*, one storey high with smooth stone walls, advanced square wings framing the central façade and decoration confined to the Gil Taboada coat of arms on the main doorway. Plays and concerts are held in the square in summer. **Plaza del Campo**, behind the palace, is lined by old houses and has a fountain at its centre. Calle de la Cruz with its bars and restaurants, and **plaza Maior**, dominated by the 18C **town hall** (*ayuntamiento*), with its gardens and esplanade, are popular with locals who come here for a stroll. The rúa do Raiña is home to the Alejo Madarro sweet shop *(confitería)*, which first opened its doors in the mid 19C.

Museo Provincial – ☎ 982 24 21 12. This museum, housed in the 18C kitchens of the former Monasterio de San Francisco, has managed to recreate the atmosphere of a traditional country kitchen similar to those found in some of the area's more remote villages. The museum is on two floors and includes one room devoted to ceramics from Sargadelos, in addition to coins and numerous exhibits from the Roman period. The former cloisters of San Francisco contain an interesting collection of sundials, as well as several altars and sarcophagi. Several entrances connect with the

Museo Nelson Zúmel, dedicated to Spanish paintings from the 19C and 20C.

Around Lugo

Santa Eulalia de Bóveda – *14km/9mi SW. Take the Orense road and turn right after 4km/2.5mi. After 2km/1.2mi turn left towards Burgo, and then right, in Poutomillos, after a further 7km/4.5mi.* ☎ 609 23 77 79.

The **palaeo-Christian monument** discovered here at the beginning of the 20C and excavated in 1924 consists of a vestibule (now open to the sky), a rectangular chamber with a round-arched niche, a rectangular pool, and frescoes of birds and leaves, doubtless of Christian origin, on the walls and vaulting. The dating and purpose of the monument continue to intrigue archaeologists.

Santa Eulalia de Bóveda

Ourense / Orense

Population: 108 382. Michelin map 571 E 6, F 6. Orense, the capital of the only Galician province without a coastline, is situated on the banks of the River Miño, 111km/69mi SE of Santiago de Compostela via the AP 53 motorway and N 525. ☐ Curros Enríquez 1 (Torre de Orense), 32003, ☎ 988 37 20 20.

Since Antiquity, Orense (Ourense in Galician) – the name is said to come from the legendary gold believed to exist in the Miño Valley – has been famous for its waters which pour out from three springs, Las Burgas, at a temperature of 65oC/150oF. The town has preserved an old bridge, Puente Romano, which dates from the 13C when it was rebuilt on Roman foundations to provide a crossing for pilgrims on their way to Santiago de Compostela.

Cathedral★

☎ 988 26 64 38. The cathedral, which took from the 12C to the 13C to build, has been constantly modified over the ages. The **Portada Sur** (South Door), in the Compostelan style, lacks a tympanum, but is profusely decorated with carvings on covings and capitals. The **Portada Norte** (North Door) has two statue columns and, beneath a great ornamental arch, a 15C Deposition framed by a Flight into Egypt and statues of the Holy Women.

The **interior** is noteworthy for its pure lines. At the end of the 15C, a Gothic-Renaissance transitional style **lantern**★ was built above the transept. The high altar has an ornate Gothic retable by Cornelius de Holanda. The 16C and 17C **Capilla del Santísimo Cristo** (Chapel of the Holy Sacrament), decorated with exuberant sculpture in the Galician Baroque style, opens off the north transept. The triple-arched **Pórtico del Paraíso**★★ (Paradise Door) at the west end, with its beautiful carvings and bright medieval colouring, illustrates the same theme as the Pórtico de la Gloria in Santiago Cathedral. The central arch shows the 24 Old Men of the Apocalypse; to the right is the Last Judgement. The pierced tympanum above, like the narthex vaulting, is 16C.

A door in the south aisle opens onto the 13C chapter house, now the **Museo Catedralicio**. Among the items displayed are church plate, statues, chasubles and a 12C travelling altar.

Museo Arqueológico y de Bellas Artes

Closed for restoration. ☎ 988 22 38 84.

The city's archaeological and fine arts museum is housed in

Ourense / Orense

J. Fiuza/MICHELIN

the former episcopal palace, whose façade, adorned with a coat of arms, looks onto the plaza Mayor. The collections inside include prehistoric specimens, cultural objects (mainly statues of warriors) and a fine arts section featuring an early-18C wood carving of the **Camino del Calvario**★ (Stations of the Cross).

Claustro de San Francisco★

Closed for restoration. ☎ 988 38 81 10. These elegant and tranquil 14C cloisters consist of horseshoe-shaped Gothic arches, embellished with diamond decoration, and resting on slender, paired columns. The simple yet refined **capitals** are adorned with vegetal and animal motifs.

Puente Romano, Ourense

Around Ourense

Monasterio de Santa María la Real de Oseira*

34km/21mi NW. Leave Orense on the N 525. After 23km/14mi turn right towards Cotelas. ☎ *988 28 20 04.*

This grandiose Cistercian monastery was founded by Alfonso VII in the middle of the 12C. It stands in an isolated position in the Arenteiro Valley, a region that once abounded in bears *(osos)* as the monastery's name suggests.

The façade (1708) consists of three sections. In a niche below the statue of Hope which crowns the doorway is the figure of a Nursing Madonna with St Bernard at her feet. Of note inside the monastery are a grand staircase and the Claustro de los Medallones (Medallion Cloisters), decorated with 40 busts of famous historical figures.

The church (12C-13C), hidden behind the Baroque façade of 1637, has retained the customary Cistercian simplicity, modified only by the frescoes in the transept which were painted in 1694.

The **chapter house**★ dates from the late 15C and early 16C and is outstanding for its beautiful vaulting of crossed ribs descending like the fronds of a palm tree onto four spiral columns.

Celanova

26km/16mi S on the OU 540. The large, imposing **monastery** (☎ 988 43 22 01) on plaza Mayor was founded in 936 by San Rosendo, Bishop of San Martín de Mondoñedo. The monastery was of huge importance for several centuries.

The **church** is a monumental late-17C edifice built in Baroque style. The coffered vaulting is decorated with geometrical designs, the cupola with volutes. An immense altarpiece (1697) occupies the back of the apse. Note also the choir stalls, Baroque in the lower part and Gothic in the upper, as well as the fine organ.

The **cloisters**★★, among the most beautiful in the region, took until the 18C to complete even though construction began in 1550. The majestic staircases here are particularly worthy of note.

The **Capilla de San Miguel**, a chapel behind the church, is one of the monastery's earliest buildings (937) and one of the rare Mozarabic monuments still in good condition.

Tour along the Río Sil★

65km/40mi E. Head along the C 536; after 6km/4mi, turn left towards Luintra and continue for a further 18km/11mi. The monastery is signposted.

Monasterio de San Estevo de Ribas de Sil – *Work to convert the building into a hotel is currently being completed; as a result the monastery is closed. Before starting your journey, check with the tourist office in Orense.* The monastery appears suddenly in a majestic **setting**★, spread over a great spur, against a background of granite mountains deeply cut by the Sil. The church's Romanesque east end remains, as do the three cloisters, built to grandiose proportions largely in the 16C, although one still has Romanesque galleries surmounted by elegant low arches.

Gargantas del Sil★ – *Return on the downhill road on the left towards the Sil (do not take the signposted turning to the embalse de San Estevo).* Two dams, one vaulted (presa de San Esteban), the other buttressed (presa de San Pedro), control the waters of the Sil which flow through deep gorges. The sides of the valley are dotted with vineyards and small villages.

Continue along the left bank of the river until you reach the N 120. Turn left towards Orense.

Pontevedra★

Population: 75 148. Michelin map 571 E 4 – for local map see Rías Bajas. Pontevedra is situated at the head of the estuary (ría) of the same name, 57km/35.5mi S of Santiago de Compostela along the AP 9 motorway. ⚑ *Gutiérrez Mellado 1 bajo, 36001 Pontevedra,* ☎ *986 85 08 14.*

Pontevedra is a quiet provincial town where life continues in an ordered and unhurried fashion. The architecture here is a pleasant mix of fine buildings, plain arcades, cobbled streets, squares embellished with the occasional stone cross, and attractive parks and gardens. The town's bars and cafés, their outdoor terraces teeming in summer, offer a cosy retreat in the cool of winter.

Old quarter★

Allow 1hr 30min. In spite of extensive development, the old quarter (*casco antiguo*), in the area between calle Michelena, calle del Arzobispo Malvar, calle Cobián and the river, has managed to survive the test of time. Here, life continues peacefully in the shadow of glazed house fronts, squares occasionally adorned with a Calvary (**plaza de la Leña**; **del Teucro**; **de Mugártegui)** and streets near the Lérez (**Pedreira**, **Real**, **San Nicolás)**. The town comes to life in **calle Sarmiento** on market days.

Plaza de la Leña★ – This is a delightful square with its asymmetrical shape, its Calvary and the beautiful façades that surround it. Two 18C mansions on the square have been converted into a museum.

Museo Provincial – ☎ 986 85 14 55. The ground floor of the museum contains prehistoric collections, in particular the **Celtic treasures★** from

Parador

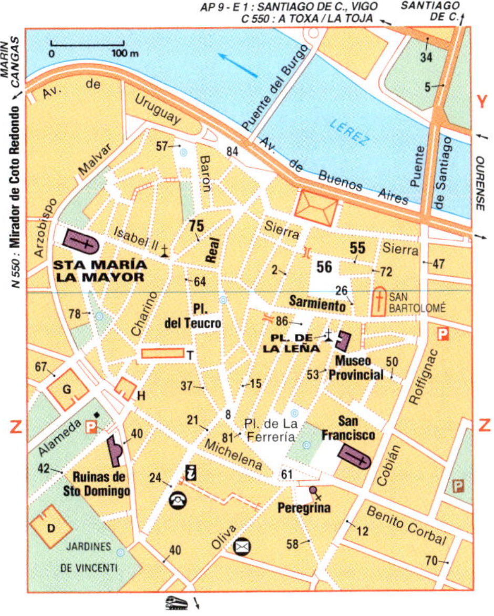

PONTEVEDRA

Benito Corbal .... **Z**
Buenos Aires (Av. de) .... **Y**
César Boente .... **Y** 2
Compostela (Av. de) .... **Y** 5
Curros Enríquez (Pl. de) ..... **Z** 8
Daniel de la Sota .... **Z** 12
Don Gonzalo .... **Z** 15
España (Pl. de) .... **Z** 18
Fernández Villaverde .... **Z** 21
General Gutiérrez Mellado . **Z** 24
Gregorio Fernández .... **YZ** 26
Juan Manuel Pintos .... **Y** 34
Manuel Quiroga .... **Z** 37
Marqués de Riestra .... **Z** 40
Michelena .... **Z**
Monte Rios (Gran Vía de) ... **Z** 42
Oliva .... **Z**
Padre Amoedo Carballo ...... **Y** 47

Padre Luis María Fernández . **Z** 50
Pasantería .... **Z** 53
Pedreira .... **Y** 55
Pedreira (Pl. de la) .... **Y** 56
Peirao (Pl. do) .... **Y** 57
Peregrina .... **Z** 58
Peregrina (Pl.) .... **Z** 61
Princesa .... **YZ** 64
Prudencio Landín Tobio ..... **Z** 67
Real .... **Y**
Sagasta .... **Z** 70
San Bartolomé (Arcos de) ... **Y** 72
San Nicolás .... **Y** 75
Santa María (Av. de) .... **Z** 78
Sarmiento .... **YZ**
Soportales de la Herrería ... **Z** 81
Valentín García
  Escudero (Pl.) .... **Y** 84
Verdura (Pl. de la) .... **Z** 86

A Golada and Caldas de Reis which date from the Bronze Age, and that of Foxados from the 2C and 1C BC, as well as the pre-1900 silverware col-lection of Fernández de la Mora y Mon, containing over 600 hand-worked pieces from a number of countries. The first floor, which is dedicated

AN IMPORTANT PORT

Pontevedra was once a busy port lying sheltered at the end of the *ría* of the same name, inhabited by fisherman and merchants who sold their preserved products in overseas markets.

The town has given rise to great sailors, including **Pedro Sarmiento**, skilled navigator of the 16C, wise cosmographer and author of *Voyage to the Magellan Straits*. The Lérez delta, however, silted up so that by the 18C Pontevedra had begun to decline and the new port at Marín started to take its place.

to paintings, has several 15C Aragonese Primitives on display.

The second mansion includes a reconstruction of a stateroom from the *Numancia*, the frigate captained by Admiral Méndez Núñez during the disastrous Battle of Callao (Peru's chief sea port) in 1866. When told that it was folly to attack a port so well defended, the admiral replied, "Spain prefers honour without ships to ships without honour." On the museum's upper floor are an interesting antique kitchen and 19C Sargadelos ceramics. A large collection of interesting pieces of jet is also on display in this building.

Iglesia de Santa María la Mayor* – ☎ *986 86 61 85*. Old alleyways and gardens surround this delightful Plateresque church built by Pontevedra's Mariners' Guild in the 16C. The **west front***, attributed to Cornelius de Holanda, is carved like an altarpiece and divided into separate superimposed registers featuring reliefs of the Dormition and Assumption of the Virgin and the Trinity. At the summit is the Crucifixion, at the centre of an openwork coping finely carved with oarsmen and fishermen hauling in their nets. A sculpture of St Jerome can be seen to one side.

The **interior** is a generally successful mingling of Gothic (notched arches), Isabelline (slender cabled columns) and Renaissance (ribbed vaulting) styles. The back of the west façade is covered in naive low reliefs of scenes from Genesis (Adam and Eve, Noah's Ark) and the New Testament.

San Francisco – The church's simply styled Gothic

J. Malburet/MICHELIN

façade, so characteristic of the mendicant orders, looks onto the gardens of **plaza de la Herrería**. The main features of interest inside the church are the three apses and the timber vaulting crowning the central nave.

Capilla de la Peregrina – This small church, with its scallop-shaped floor plan and convex façade, dates from the end of the 18C. Its interior contains a statue of the patron saint of Pontevedra.

Ruinas de Santo Domingo – ☎ 986 85 14 55. These ruins are a perfect example of medieval romanticism. The church's Gothic east end still remains, surrounded by five elegant apses with lofty windows overgrown with ivy. Arranged inside is a display of Roman steles, Galician coats of arms and tombs of artisans, represented by their tools, and of noblemen, including Payo Gómez de Sotomayor, ambassador to the Court of Persia under under Enrique III.

Around Pontevedra

Mirador de Coto Redondo★★ – *14km/9mi S on the N 550. Take the Vigo road; after 6km/4mi, turn right towards the Lago Castiñeiras and then follow the signposts.*
Access to this viewpoint is through attractive woods of eucalyptus and pine. The reward at the summit is a wonderful **view**★★ of the surrounding area.

Plaza de la Leña

Rías Altas ★

Michelin map 571 A 5-7, B 4-8, C 2-5, D 2 – Lugo, A Coruña/ La Coruña. The easiest route to the Rías Altas from Santiago de Compostela is via A Coruña/ La Coruña (or Ferrol). ⓘ *Ferrol: praza de Camilo José Cela, ☎ 981 31 11 79; Foz: avenida de Lugo, 1, ☎ 982 14 06 75; Mondoñedo: praza de la Catedral 34, ☎ 982 50 71 77; Ribadeo: praza de España, ☎ 982 12 86 89; Viveiro: avenida de Ramón Canosa, ☎ 982 56 08 79.*

The northern coast of Galicia from Ribadeo to Cabo Finisterre is generally low-lying. The bare, smooth rocks and granite houses with slate roofs bear witness to a climate that can be harsh, although the area is popular with visitors in summer attracted by the fascinating scenery and charming sandy creeks.

The Rías Altas comprise a succession of deep inlets *(rías)* backed by thick forests of pine and eucalyptus. The inlets below are described from east to west.

Ría de Ribadeo

The ría de Ribadeo is formed by the estuary of the Eo, a river popular for salmon fishing. After a headlong course, the river, which forms the border between Galicia and

C. Jaffres/MICHELIN

Playa de las Catedrales, Ribadeo

B. Brillion/MICHELIN

Plaza de la Catedral, Mondoñedo

Asturias, slackens its pace to wind gently between the wide green banks of its lower valley. The old port of **Ribadeo**, at its mouth, is now an important regional centre and summer resort. A beautiful **view**★ can be enjoyed up the estuary from the bridge across the mouth of the *ría*.

Ría de Foz

Foz, at the mouth of the inlet of the same name, is a small port with a coastal fishing fleet. Its two attractive Atlantic beaches are popular in summer.

Iglesia de San Martín de Mondoñedo – *Take the Mondoñedo road, then immediately turn right.* ☏ 982 14 06 75. This isolated hilltop church was once part of an old monastery which was an episcopal seat until 1112, when this was transferred to Mondoñedo. The style of the church is archaic and, most unusually in this region, shows no sign of Compostelan influence. The east end, decorated with Lombard bands, is supported by massive buttresses. Inside, the transept **capitals**★ are naively carved and rich in anecdotal detail: the one to the right, illustrating the parable of the rich man who allows Lazarus to die of hunger, shows the table overflowing with food while a dog beneath it is licking Lazarus's feet as he lies stretched out on the ground; those to the left show Visigothic influence in their use of plant motifs.

Mondoñedo – *23km/14mi SW along the N 634.* Mondoñedo rises out of the hollow of a lush, well cultivated valley. The streets of the old town are lined with stylish white-walled houses ornamented with armorial bearings and wrought-iron balconies. The cathedral square is particularly delightful with its arcades and *solanas* (glassed-in galleries).

The immense façade of the **cathedral**★ combines the

C. Jaffres/MICHELIN   **Cabo Ortegal**

Gothic grace of the three large portal arches and the rose window, all dating from the 13C, with the grandiose Baroque style of the towers added in the 18C.

On the sober **interior**, transitional Romanesque in style, the most noteworthy features include a series of late-14C frescoes one above the other (below the organ) illustrating the Massacre of the Innocents and the Life of St Peter; the Rococo retable at the high altar; and a polychrome wood statue of the Virgin in the south ambulatory, known as the English Virgin (the statue was brought from St Paul's, in London, to Mondoñedo in the 16C). Off the south aisle is the burial niche of Bishop Juan Muñoz who gave the church its present façade. The classical cloisters were added in the 17C.

Ría de Viveiro

Sea, countryside and mountains combine in a varied landscape, a coastline of white sandy beaches and lofty headlands celebrated by **Nicomedes Pastor Díaz**, a 19C politician and poet.

All that **Viveiro** retains of its town walls is the Puerta de Carlos V (Charles V Gateway), emblazoned with the emperor's arms. On the 4th Sunday in August, visitors from all over Galicia come here for the local Naseiro Romería festival.

Ría de Santa María de Ortigueira

The *ría* is deep and surrounded by green hills. The quayside of the port of **Ortigueira** is bordered by attractive gardens.

Ría de Cedeira

This small, deeply enclosed *ría* is renowned for its beautiful beaches. The road affords good **views** of **Cedeira** and the surrounding countryside.

Ría de Ferrol

The *ría* forms a magnificent natural harbour accessed via a narrow 6km/4mi channel guarded by two forts. As a result of its superb location and favourable position for trade with America, in the 18C King Ferdinand VI and King Charles III decided to make the port of **Ferrol** a naval base. The symmetry of the town plan evident in the old quarter dates from the same period.

Today, Ferrol is one of Spain's major naval bases and is also a dockyard.

Betanzos

Betanzos★, a one-time port which has now silted up as a result of alluvium from the Mandeo river, stands at the end of the *ría* of the same name. Built on a hill, its old quarter has retained substantial reminders of its former prosperity in the form of three richly ornamented Gothic churches and its steep streets and old houses with glassed-in balconies.

Iglesia de Santa María del Azogue★ – ☎ 981 77 07 02. The gracefully asymmetrical façade of this 14C-15C church is given character by a projecting central bay pierced by a rose window and a portal with sculptured covings. Niches on either

C. Jaffres/MICHELIN

Castillo de la Palma alongside the ría of Ferrol

C. Jaffres/MICHELIN

side contain archaic statues of the Virgin and the Archangel Gabriel, symbolising the Annunciation. Inside, three aisles of equal height create an effect of spaciousness.

Iglesia de San Francisco★ – ☏ 981 77 01 10. This Franciscan monastery church, in the shape of a Latin Cross embellished with a graceful Gothic east end, was built in 1387 by the powerful Count Fernán Pérez de Andrade. It is chiefly remarkable for the many tombs aligned along its walls, the carved decoration on its ogives and chancel arches and the wild boar sculpted in the most unexpected places. Beneath the gallery to the left of the west door is the **monumental sepulchre★** of the founder, supported by a wild boar and a bear, his heraldic beasts. Scenes of the hunt adorn the sides of the tomb; his hounds lie couched at his feet, while at his head an angel greets his soul.

Iglesia de Santiago – The interior of this church, built in the 15C by the tailors' guild, resembles that of the Iglesia de Santa María. Above the main door is a carving of St James *Matamoros* or Slayer of the Moors.

The 16C **ayuntamiento** (town hall) abutting the east end is embellished with an arcade and a fine sculpted coat of arms.

Ría de La Coruña

(see p 74)

Costa de la Muerte

The wild coastline between La Coruña and Cabo Finisterre, known as the Coast of Death, is characterised by a landscape that is both harsh and majestic. Over the centuries, numerous ships have run aground or been smashed to pieces against its rocks.

Tucked away in its more sheltered coves, however, are small fishing villages such as **Malpica de Bergantiño**, protected by the Cabo de San Adrián (opposite the Islas Si-sargas, islands home to a bird sanctuary), and **Camariñas**, famous for its bobbin-lace.

Cabo Finisterre (Cabo Fisterra)★ – Corcubión★, near Cape Finisterre, is an attractive old harbour town of emblazoned houses with glassed-in balconies. The **coast road★** to the cape looks down over the Bahía de Cabo Finisterre, a bay enclosed by three successive mountain chains. The lighthouse on the headland commands a fine **view★** of the Atlantic and the bay.

B. Brillion/MICHELIN

Corcubión

Rías Bajas ★★

Michelin map 571 D 2-3, E 2-3; F 3-4 – A Coruña/La Coruña, Pontevedra. The Ría de Muros i Noia can be reached from Santiago along the AC 543 (Noia is located 37km/23mi from the city); the other inlets are accessible via the AP 9 motorway.
🛈 *Baiona: Paseo de Ribeira, 36300 Pontevedra, ☎ 986 68 70 67; Sanxenxo: Madrid, 36960 Pontevedra, ☎ 986 72 02 85; Vigo: Dársena de la Estación Marítima de Trasantlánticos, 36201 Pontevedra, ☎ 986 43 05 77; Tui: Puente de Tripes, 36700 Pontevedra, ☎ 986 60 17 89.*

The Rías Bajas is Galicia's most attractive region, enhanced by the friendliness of its people and and the excellent local cuisine, particularly its wonderful seafood. Much of its day-to-day existence is determined by its links with the sea, which cuts numerous paths inland through deep inlets providing safe anchorage for local sailors. The beaches and resorts of the Rías Bajas are popular summer attractions in their own right, catering to a predominantly Spanish clientele.

The Rías Bajas is formed by four inlets: the ría de Muros y Noia, the smallest, forming the estuary of the River

Port of Muros

Tambre; the ría de Arousa, the delta of the River Ulla and separated from the for- mer by the Barbanza Penin- sula, from where the Mirador de la Curota provides stun-

Origins

The *rías* are river valleys that have been invaded by the sea. In the case of the Galician coast, its formation is the result of tectonic movements which caused the collapse of the coastline and the advance of the sea.

A. González/MICHELIN

View from the Mirador de la Curota

ning views; the ría de Pontevedra, surrounded by delightful beaches; and the ría de Vigo, with the Islas Cíes at its mouth.

Ría de Muros y Noia★★

1 *From Muros to Ribeira 71km/44mi – about 1hr 15min*

This *ría* is especially delightful for its wild scenery. The wooded northern bank is particularly attractive.

Muros is a typical fishing port. **Noia**, on the opposite side of the inlet, is known for its main square facing out to sea, and the Gothic **Iglesia de San Martín**★, with its magnificently carved portal and rose window.

Ría de Arousa

2 *From Ribeira to A Toxa 115km/ 71mi – about 3hr*

This *ría*, at the mouth of the River Ulla, is the largest and most indented of the area's inlets.

Ribeira – This fishing port is home to numerous large canning factories.

Mirador de la Curota★★ – *10km/6mi from A Pobra do Caramiñal.* From a height of 498m/1 634ft there is a magnificent **panorama**★★ of the four inlets of the Rías Bajas. On a clear day the view extends from Cabo Finisterre to the River Miño.

Padrón – According to tradition, it was in this village

A. González/MICHELIN

Iglesia de Padrón

A. González/MICHELIN

Iglesia San Benito, Cambados

that the legendary boat bringing St James to Spain came ashore. The boat's mooring stone *(pedrón)* can be seen beneath the altar in the *iglesia parroquial* (parish church) near the bridge. The town is also renowned for its green peppers.

Iria Flavia *(at the exit to the town, heading north along the N 550)* is home to the **Fundación Camilo José Cela**; the Iglesia de Santa María de Andina, with its Romanesque portal and various open-air tombs; a small sacred art museum; as well as the house, now converted into a **museum** (☎ 981 81 12 04), once occupied by the poet **Rosalía de Castro** (1837-85).

The **Santuario de A Escravitude**, a monumental construction built in Baroque and neo-Classical style next to a fountain which according to tradition has therapeutic qualities, is located a further 5km/3mi along the same road.

Vilagarcía de Arousa – The maritime promenade in this popular resort is bordered by attractive gardens. The Convento de Vista Alegre, founded in 1648, stands on the outskirts of the town along the Cambados road. This old Galician mansion *(pazo)* is embellished with square towers, various coats of arms and pointed merlons.

Mirador de Lobeira★ – *4km/2.5mi S. In Cornazo follow a signposted forest track to the viewpoint.* The view from the mirador encompasses the whole *ría* and the hills inland.

Cambados★ – The **plaza de Fefiñanes★** stands at the northern entrance to the town. This magnificent square is lined on two sides by the façade of the pazo de Fefiñanes, on the third by the 17C Iglesia de San Benito, and on the fourth by a row of arcaded houses. Also worthy of note on the other side of the village are the romantic ruins of **Santa Mariña de Dozo**, a 12C parish church which is now a cemetery. Cambados is the place to try Albariño, a light and fruity white wine.

A Toxa★ – A sick donkey abandoned on the island by its owner was the first living creature to discover the health-giving properties of the spring in A Toxa. The stream has run dry but the pine-covered island in its wonderful **setting★★** remains a delightfully restful place.

The seaside resort and fishing harbour of **O Grove** on the other side of the causeway is renowned for its seafood.

Aquariumgalicia – ☺ *From O Grove head towards San Vicente and turn off at Reboredo.* ☎ *986 73 15 15.* This, the only aquarium in Galicia, has over 15 000 exhibits representing more than 150 species on display in 18 tanks which recreate different marine habitats. The complex also includes a marine farm where

Isla de La Toja

A. González/MICHELIN

Views of the ría from the A Granxa belvedere

species of commercial interest, such as the unusual turbot and the gilthead, are bred.
The **road**★ from A Toxa to Canelas enjoys extensive views of sand dunes and rock-enclosed beaches such as **La Lanzada**.

Ría de Pontevedra★

③ *From A Toxa to Hío 62km/ 39mi – about 3hr*

Sanxenxo – This resort, which is particularly popular in summer, enjoys one of the best climates in Galicia.

Monasterio de Armenteira – ☎ *986 71 83 00.* In Samieira a small road leads to this Cistercian monastery, where a 12C church and 17C classical-style cloisters can still be visited.

Combarro★ – This typical fishing village with its winding alleyways has preserved a number of calvaries and **drying sheds**★ *(hórreos)* along its seafront.

Pontevedra★ – *See p 90*

Marín – Marín is home to the headquarters of Spain's Escuela Naval Militar (Military Naval Academy).

Hío – The village is famous for its **Calvary**★, one of the most beautiful in the whole of Galicia.

Ría de Vigo★★

④ *From Hío to Baiona 70km/ 43mi – about 3hr*

Although narrower than the ría de Arousa, the Vigo inlet is deeper and more sheltered,

C. Jaffres/MICHELIN

Islas Cíes

with protection provided by the offshore Islas Cíes. The landscape is particularly beautiful around Domaio, where the steep, wooded banks are drawn together to form a narrow channel covered with mussel beds. The city of Vigo, a white swathe on the hillside on the far side of the inlet, is visible from Cangas and Moaña.

Vigo – *Michelin Vigo city plan 19080.* Vigo, Spain's principal transatlantic port, is home to the country's largest fishing fleet and is one of its most important industrial and commercial centres. Legend has it that treasure dating from the time of Philip V lies at the bottom of the inlet. Vigo's **setting*** is out-standing: the city is built in a natural amphitheatre on the south bank of the *ría* and surrounded by parks and pinewoods. Magnificent **views**** of Vigo and its bay can be enjoyed from the colina del Castro, a hill behind the city. Berbés, Vigo's oldest quarter and home to a district populated by fishermen and sailors, is particularly attractive. Beside it stands the unusual A Pedra market, selling oysters which can be tasted in the neighbourhood's numerous bars.

The **Museo del Mar** (☎ 986 24 76 95) has been built at the scenic punta do Muiño, with its impressive views of the inlet. Designed by the architects Aldo Rossi and César

GETTING TO THE CÍES ISLANDS
From June to September, daily boat services operate from Cangas and Vigo (journey time: 30min). For information, call ☎ 986 22 52 72.

Portela, this maritime museum highlights Vigo's relationship with the sea.

Islas Cíes★ – *Access by boat from the port of Vigo.* The beautiful archipelago of crystalline water and immaculate white sand guards the entrance to the ría de Vigo. The archipelago, a bird sanctuary, was decreed a nature reserve in 1980. Today it forms part of the **Parque Nacional de las Islas Atlánticas de Galicia**, created in 2002. The archipelago comprises three islands: Monteagudo, El Faro and San Martiño. The first two are linked via a sandy beach, the playa de Rodas.

Mirador la Madroa★★ – *6km/4mi. Exit Vigo along the airport road. After 3.5km/2mi turn left, following signposts to the "parque zoológico" (zoo).* The esplanade commands a fine **view★★** of Vigo and the *ría*.

The Alcabre, Samil and Canido beaches extend to the south of Vigo.

Panxón – *14km/9mi SW along the C 550.* This seaside resort stands at the foot of Monte Ferro.

Playa América – This popular, elegant resort is located on the curve of the bay.

Baiona★ – It was here, on 10 March 1493, that the cara-

A. González/MICHELIN

The port of Baiona

A. González/MICHELIN

Monasterio de Santa María la Real, Oia

vel *Pinta* – one of the three vessels in Christopher Columbus's fleet – captained by **Martín Alonso Pinzón**, sailed into Baiona bringing news of the discovery of the New World.

Today, Baiona has developed into a lively summer resort with a harbour for fishing boats and pleasure craft fronted by a promenade of terrace cafés. In the old quarter houses can still be seen with coats of arms and typical glassed-in balconies. The **ex-colegiata** (former collegiate church) at the top of the town was built in a transitional Romanesque-Gothic style between the 12C and 14C. Symbols on the arches of chisels, axes and knives represent the various guilds that contributed to the building of the church. Note also the stone pulpit dating from the 14C.

Monterreal – ☎ 986 35 63 85. The Catholic Monarchs had a defensive wall built around the Monterreal promontory at the beginning of the 16C. The fort within, which became the governor's residence, has since been converted into a parador, surrounded by a pleasant pine forest. It is well worth taking a **walk around the battle-ments★** *(about 30min)*, rising abruptly above the rocks, to admire the splendid **views★★** of the bay, Monte Ferro, the Islas Estela, and the coast with its sandy coves stretching south to the cabo Silleiro headland.

The road from Baiona to Tui★

5 *58km/36mi.* The coast between Baiona and A Guarda is a relatively flat area indented by the sea.

Oia – The houses in this fishing village are clustered around the former Cistercian abbey of **Santa María la Real**

with its Baroque façade. Wild horses can be seen roaming on the gently sloping green hills on the opposite side of the road. Festivals known as *curros*, during which wild foals are rounded up for branding, are held in the area on some Sundays in May and June.

A Guarda/La Guarda – This small fishing village stands at the extreme southern end of the Galician coastline. To the south, **Monte Santa Tecla★** (341m/1 119ft) rises above the mouth of the Miño, affording fine **views★★** from the top *(follows signs to the Citania de Santa Trega)*. On the slopes are the extensive remains of a **Celtic city**, testimony to human habitation from the Bronze Age to the 3C AD. Two round huts with stone walls and thatched roofs have been reconstructed by the side of the road.

Castle ruins, Monte de Santa Tecla

A. González/MICHELIN

View of A Garda from Monte de Santa Tecla

From A Guarda, the PO 552 heads inland parallel to the River Miño.

Tui/Tuy★ – Tui is located in a striking **setting**★ just across the border from Portugal. Its old quarter, facing the Portuguese fortress of Valença do Minho, stretches down the rocky hillside to the right bank of the River Miño. The **Parque de Santo Domingo**, home to a 14C Gothic church of the same name, commands a good view of Tui and the Portuguese coast.

Since 1884, when a bridge was built across the Miño by Gustave Eiffel, Tui has served as a gateway to Portugal.

This historic town is one of the oldest in Galicia; its emblazoned houses and narrow stepped alleys climbing towards the cathedral testifying to its rich past.

Without doubt, the **cathedral**★ is Tui's most important monument (☎ 986 60 05 11). As a result of frequent attacks by the Portuguese, the city resolved to transform the building into a fortress, adding towers and crenellations. Romanesque and Gothic in style, the cathedral was consecrated in 1232. The Romanesque north door, marked only by arches cut into the wall stone, is more austere than the west door, to which a magnificent portal, ogival in style, was added in the 15C. While remaining ostensibly defensive in character, the cathedral's main **portal**★ is highly decorative with eight archivolts adorned with reliefs; reliefs are also found on the tympanum, depicting the Virgin Mary, Mother of God; and the city of Jerusalem, appearing as backdrop to the Adoration of the Magi and Shepherds.

Inside, note the impressive reinforcing beams added to the cathedral in the 15C and 18C to compensate for the slant of the pillars. The transept plan of the three aisles is Compostelan in style; in Spain, this is found only in this church and in Santiago de Compostela. Modifications were made to the chapels from the 16C to the 18C. The carvings on the choir stall recount the life and miracles of San Telmo, patron saint of Tuy.

The sentry path above the wide galleries of the **cloisters**, soberly decorated in Cistercian style, commands impressive views of the river valley, with Portugal on the opposite bank.

Another building worthy of mention is the **Capilla de San Telmo**. This Portuguese-style reliquary chapel has been built below the cathedral on the site of the house of **San Pedro González Telmo**, a Dominican born in Frómista who lived in Tuy and died here in 1240. Pilgrims can visit the alcove in the crypt where the saint died *(entrance on rúa do Corpo Santo).*

Catedral, Tui

Directory

Celtic settlement, Rías Bajas

Transport

Airport – The city's airport is located 11km/7mi to the east along the N 547 towards Lugo. ☎ 981 59 74 00 and 981 59 75 00.

Reservations: ☎ 902 34 34 34

Trains – Railway station: rúa do Hórreo, ☎ 981 50 60 50. Santiago has several departures every day to other large towns and cities around Galicia. The city is also served by two daily services to Madrid as well as links with Portugal (via Vigo) and France (via Barcelona).

RENFE (Spanish State Railways): 902 24 02 02 and 981 52 02 02.

City buses – For information, call ☎ 901 12 00 54. Santiago's bus network covers the whole city, including services between the city centre and all suburban areas. A single ticket costs €0.80.

Taxis – ☎ 981 56 10 28.

Sightseeing

"Compostela 48 horas" tourist card – This good-value card, on sale in the city's tourist office, is valid for 48 hours and allows free use of all public transport, as well as offering a 50% discount on tourist transport (bus and train). It also provides free admission or significant discounts on entry to the city's museums, between 15 and 50% discount for cultural events, as well as a 10% discount in numerous restaurants and shops.

Guided tours of the historic centre – The city's association of professional tour guides offers 2hr guided tours of the city's main sites and monuments. For information, call ☎ 981 569 890. Meeting-point: plaza de Platerías, beneath the arcades of the Banco de España.

Dolmen, Axeitos

Where to Eat

The restaurants listed in this section have been chosen for their surroundings, ambience, typical dishes or unusual character. Prices specified correspond to the average cost of both an inexpensive and expensive meal and are given as a guideline only. Restaurants are classified into three categories based on price:

- Budget: under €15
- Moderate: between €15 and €30
- Expensive: over €30

O Dezaseis – *Rúa de San Pedro, 16 – ☎ 981 57 76 33 – Reservation recommended – €11/24.* Near the Porta do Camiño and the Museo do Pobo Galego, this restaurant has carved an impressive niche in Santiago gastronomy with its delicious tapas and excellent wines, which can also be enjoyed beneath the vines on the terrace. Attractive decor of wood and local stone.

Bierzo Enxebre – *Rúa Troia, 10 – ☎ 981 58 19 09 – Closed Tue – €10/20.* This welcoming restaurant in a well-known street in the old quarter is rustic in style with stone walls and wood ceilings. As the name would suggest, culinary prominence here is given to specialities from the Bierzo region.

El Asesino – *Praça da Universidade, 16 – ☎ 981 58 15 68 – Closed Sun and Christmas – €15/25* – A Santiago institution renowned for its home cooking and good value-for-money. According to local lore, the name of the restaurant derived from a strange event in which a cook was seen chasing a chicken knife in hand, only to be reproached by students from the nearby university who accused him of being an *asesino* (murderer).

San Clemente – *San Clemente, 6 – ☎ 981 58 08 82 – Closed Mon – ▤ – €28/36.* Very close to the cathedral but in a quiet part of the city off the tourist track, serving what have become legendary fish dishes.

Casa Marcelo – *Rúa Hortas, 1 – ☎ 981 55 85 80 – Closed Sun, Mon, Tue, 1-15 Feb and 1-15 Oct – ▤ – €31.* This charming restaurant just off plaza del Obradoiro has a deserved reputation for its innovative cuisine. Just the one menu, but well-balanced and varied. A pleasant dining environment, splendid wine list and excellent value for money.

Toñi Vicente – *Rosalía de Castro, 24 – ☎ 981 59 41 00 – Closed Sun, 15-30 May and Christmas – ▤ – €46/52.* Located just a couple of minutes to the southwest of the old quarter, this high-class restaurant is one of the best exponents of Galician cuisine, with traditional dishes that incorporate the latest creative trends from the world of gastronomy. The elegant, classic dining room is a fusion of stucco and stone walls and contemporary artwork.

In A Coruña/La Coruña

Coral – *Callejón de la Estacada, 9 – ☎ 981 20 05 69 – Closed Sun – ▤ – €23.55/35.55.* Another restaurant popular with locals for its high-quality, original cuisine and professionalism. The decor here is an attractive mix of stone and wood.

Domus – *Ángel Rebollo (Domus-Casa del Hombre) – ☎ 981 20 11 36 – Closed Mon and Feb – ▤ – €26.03.* Located inside the Museo Domus, but with a separate entrance. The restaurant's main feature is its attractive glazed dining room with one side enclosed by natural rock and another enjoying superb sea views. The modern decor is the perfect foil for traditional cuisine enhanced by the chef's creativity.

In Lugo

Mesón de Alberto – *Cruz, 4 –* 982 22 83 10 *– Closed Sun –* approx. €33. A good location in the old quarter. Bar at the entrance, plus an attractive, classically styled dining room on the first floor offering a predominanty regional menu peppered with a few international dishes.

In Ourense/Orense

Hotel-Restaurante Zarampallo – *Hermanos Villar, 19 –* 988 23 00 08 *– Restaurant: Closed Sun evening –* €29. Recommended for its excellent location in the old part of the city and first and foremost for its high-quality international menu. If you're planning on staying here, the rooms are basic but comfortable.

In Pontevedra

Rianxo – *Plaza de la Leña, 6 –* 986 85 52 11 *– Restaurant closed Sun –* €15/22. Rianxo is located in a delightful square right in the heart of the city's old quarter. Tapas bar at the entrance, with a pleasant dining room decorated in regional style on the first floor. A recommended address for reasonably priced Galician cuisine.

In Rías Altas

O'Centolo – *Bajada del Puerto – Fisterra –* 981 74 04 52 *– Close Á 22 Dec-22 Jan –* €24/36T. This popular rectaurant has builï up a faithful following of custoxers who come her´ to enjoy high-quality fish and seafood. Large bar area with a well-stocked fish tank, plus a spacious dining room on the first floor which, despite being somewhat functional, enjoys good views of the port.

Hostal-Restaurante As Garzas – *Porto Barizo, 40 – Malpica de Bergantiños – 7km/4.5mi SW towards Barizo –* 981 72 17 65 *– Closed Mon, Tue evening, Wed evening and Thu evening (except in summer, bank holidays and days preceding bank holidays) –* €28/37. As you would expect, the menu here is strongly influenced by the sea. The building is a mix of whitewash and slate, with a glass-fronted dining room offering good views overlooking the sea. The rooms in the hotel are both pleasant and comfortable.

In Rías Bajas

Tasca Típica – *Cantón, 15 – Noia –* 981 82 12 70 *– €12/21.* This old stone building in the centre of Noia has been converted into a typical bar serving tapas and a good-value daily menu. In fine weather, customers can also eat on the terrace.

Anduriña – *Calvo Sotelo, 58 – A Guarda –* 986 61 11 08 *– Closed 3-2/ Nov –* €24/30. Despite its simple appearance, this well-known local restaurant has an excellent menu, including reasonably priced fish.

La Oca – *Purificación Saavedra, 8 (opposite the Teis market) – Vigo –* 986 37 12 55 *– Closed Sat, Sun, Mon evening and Tue evening, Holy Week and 3 weeks in Aug –* €24/30. Don't be put off by the slightly out-of-the-way location or the neglected façade of this small family-run restaurant, as the food here is innovative and creative with notable French influence. A true pleasure for the palate!

Posta do Sol – *Ribeira de Fefiñans, 22 – Cambados –* 986 54 22 85 *– Closed 15-31 Jan, 15-31 Oct and Wed (except June-Dec) –* €24/35.50. This charming restaurant occupies a building that was once a bar. The dining room, with added warmth provided by the fireplace, is decorated with numerous Galician touches, although the most valuable feature is undoubtedly the Camariñas lace embellishing the curtains. The menu here focuses heavily on fish and seafood.

⊖⊜ **Casa Ramallo** – *Castro, 5 – Rois – 4km al N de Padrón por la AC 301 – ☎ 981 80 41 80 – Closed Mon and Christmas – ▤ – Reservation recommended – €24.60.* This small, family-run hotel has an excellent reputation locally for its delicious home cooking, in particular its stews, meat dishes and seafood. Highly recommended.

*T*apas

It is rare for tapas bars to list prices. Tapas or the larger *raciones* can vary enormously from one bar to the next, although as a general rule the standard is generally good, with prices rarely exceeding €15 per person for an informal meal.

Rúa do Franco – This lively street in the old quarter is the main area for bars and cafés in the city, and is popular with students and visitors alike.

Adega Abrigadorio – *Carrera del Conde, 5 – ☎ 981 56 31 63 – ▱.* This bar of long-standing tradition near the parque de la Alameda serves a good selection of *chorizos* and cured meats to a backdrop of exposed stone, wood barrels and even a small mill.

La Bodeguilla de San Roque – *San Roque, 13 – ☎ 981 56 43 79.* Despite its simple appearance, this *bodega* has earned a good reputation for its scrambled egg dishes, *chorizos* and wines. If you prefer something more substantial, there's also a pleasant restaurant on the first floor.

*W*here to Stay

Hotels listed below are divided into three categories based on the price of a single room, excluding VAT (7%), and have been chosen for their location, comfort, good value-for-money, and in some cases, their particular charm. The two prices listed under each hotel represent the cost of a single room in low season and a double room in high season.

- ⊖ Budget: under €50
- ⊖⊜ Moderate: between €50 and €80
- ⊖⊜⊜ Expensive: over €80

⊖ **Hostal Mapoula** – *Entremurallas, 10, 3° – ☎ 981 58 01 24 – 12 rooms – €27/37.* A small, family-run *hostal* in a narrow street in the old quarter, near praça do Toural. Nothing luxurious, but good service and clean rooms with en-suite bathrooms. A recommended choice, both for its location and value for money.

⊖ **Costa Vella** – *Porta da Pena, 17 – ☎ 981 56 95 30 – 14 rooms – €45/64 – ▱ €5.* This small hotel enjoys a superb location close to the Monasterio de San Martín Pinario. Pleasant small garden, plus attractively decorated guestrooms, four of which benefit from fantastic views.

⊖ **Entrecercas** – *Entrecercas, 11 – ☎ 981 57 11 51 – 7 rooms – €45/65 (including breakfast).* A stone house harbouring several centuries of history is the setting for this small hotel in the city's old quarter. Although on the cramped side, the bedrooms are well-maintained and attractively furnished.

⊖⊖ **Hotel San Clemente** – *San Clemente, 28 –* ☎ *902 40 58 58 – 10 rooms – €64.20/80.25 –* ☕ *€5.35.* The San Clemente enjoys an enviable location a couple of minutes' walk from the plaza del Obradoiro. With its ideal size, sympathetically decorated rooms based on brick and wood, and moderate prices, the hotel comes highly recommended.

⊖⊖ **Casa Grande de Cornide** – *Cornide – Teo-Casalonga – 11.5km/7mi SW of Santiago along the N 550 towards Padrón –* ☎ *981 80 55 99 – Closed Jan –* 🅿 *– 10 rooms – €60/80 –* ☕ *6€.* For those who prefer peace and quiet away from the city, this large, traditional-style Galician house offers the perfect solution. The decor and furnishings are a pleasant fusion of the classic and the modern, creating a comfortable, cosy atmosphere. In summer, guests can take advantage of the pool in the lovely garden surrounding the house.

⊖⊖ **Airas Nunes** – *Rúa do Vilar, 17 –* ☎ *902 40 58 58 – Closed Jan –* 🅿 *– 10 rooms – €69.55/85.60 –* ☕ *€6.42.* This compact hotel occupies a 17C arcaded building on rúa do Vilar, one of the most typical streets in Santiago's old quarter. The ten rooms, divided between three floors, are crowned by wooden beams and furnished with antiques.

⊖⊖⊖ **Virxe da Cerca** – *Virxe da Cerca, 27 –* ☎ *981 56 93 50 –* ▤ *– 43 rooms – €90.95/101.65 –* ☕ *€8.50.* This charming hotel located opposite the historical quarter has two sections: one occupying a building dating from the 18C, the other a more modern addition. The rooms in the older section, with their stone walls and period furniture, are perhaps preferable. Pleasant garden.

⊖⊖⊖ **Parador Hostal dos Reis Católicos** – *Plaza del Obradoiro, 1 –* ☎ *981 58 22 00 –* ▤ ♿ *– 131 rooms from €178.10 –* ☕ *€12.80.* The former Royal Hospital founded by the Catholic Monarchs in 1499 has now been converted into a luxury parador. Particularly worthy of note are its inner *patios* which trace the typology of hospitals in the 16C. Elegant rooms, some with four-poster beds.

In A Coruña/La Coruña

⊖ **Hostal Mar del Plata** – *Paseo de Ronda, 58 –* ☎ *981 25 79 62 – 27 rooms – €42 –* ☕ *€2.50.* This simple and functional family-run hotel is located just out of the city centre, near the Riazor football stadium, home of Deportivo La Coruña. The rooms here are unpretentious, but perfectly acceptable, some with sea views.

⊖⊖ **Plaza** – *Av. Fernández Latorre, 45 –* ☎ *981 29 01 11 –* ▤ ♿ *– 84 rooms – €72/96 –* ☕ *€7.20 – Restaurant €10.* The Plaza is minimalist in design with attractive decor based on pure lines and bright tones. The hotel's public areas are on the small side, although the guest rooms are contemporary in style with designer bathrooms.

In Lugo

⊖⊖ **Méndez Núñez** – *Raiña, 1 –* ☎ *982 23 07 11 –* ▤ ♿ *– 86 rooms – €50/63 –* ☕ *€7.* This hotel's major selling point is its location on a pedestrian street within the city walls. A traditional feel, which is gradually being updated to offer enhanced facilities and levels of comfort.

In Ourense/Orense

⊖ **Hotel Altiana** – *Ervedelo, 14 –* ☎ *988 37 09 52 – 32 rooms – €27/40 (including VAT) –* ☕ *€3.80.* Located near the cathedral and calle Progreso, the Altiana is a simple but friendly place to stay for those on a budget. Although far from luxurious, the bedrooms all have TVs and en-suite bathrooms and are reasonably priced.

In Pontevedra

● **Ruas** – *Sarmiento, 20 – ☎ 986 84 64 16 – 🖼 – 22 rooms – €38/58 – ☕ €5*. This attractive, arcaded stone building is also home to a busy café. Although simply furnished, the bedrooms are reasonably comfortable, with wooden floors and modern bathrooms.

In Rías Altas

●● **Pazo da Trave** – *Galdo – 3.5km/2mi S of Viveiro along the C 640 – ☎ 982 59 81 63 – 🅿 – 18 rooms – €45.08/90.15 – ☕ €7.21 – Restaurant €31.25.* A stylish, tastefully furnished hotel in an old stone house with a garden dating back to the 15C. Inside, the predominant theme is wood, as seen in the flooring, exposed beams and furniture. Comfortable bedrooms and a good restaurant.

In Rías Bajas

● **Casa do Torno** – *Lugar do Torno, 1 – Noia – 1.1km/0.7mi S of Noia along the Boiro road. – ☎ 981 84 20 74 – 8 rooms – €34.32/50.47 – ☕ €4.21.* A rural hotel in an unpretentious whitewashed village house with a garden at the rear. Cosy rooms with wooden floors and antique furniture. Although on the small side, the bathrooms are pleasant with good attention to detail. The perfect base for a few days of relaxation.

●● **Hotel Convento de San Benito** – *Pl. de San Benito – A Guarda – ☎ 986 61 11 66 – Closed Jan – 23 rooms – €48/70 – ☕ €5.* This former convent near the fishing port of A Guarda was founded in the 16C and originally housed an order of Benedictine nuns. A haven of peace and quiet with simple yet elegant rooms and fine classical-style cloisters.

●● **Hotel Pazo de Mendoza** – *Elduayen, 1 – Baiona – ☎ 986 38 50 14 – 11 rooms – €56/85 – ☕ €4.50 – Restaurant €10.50.* A modern hotel built within the walls of an 18C house facing the sea in the centre of Baiona. The rooms are comfortable and well-furnished with attractive wooden floors. The creative restaurant menu is based on high-quality local products.

●● **Pazo de Hermida** – *Trasmuro, 21 – Lestrove – 1km/0.6mi SW of Padrón – ☎ 981 81 71 10 – Closed 21 Dec-7 Jan – 🅿 – 6 rooms – €79 – ☕ €6.* This Galician manor house *(pazo)*, built in the 17C above two former defensive towers, was for a short time home to the 19C poet Rosalía de Castro, who was undoubtedly attracted here by the tranquillity of the setting. Comfortable rooms and a highly recommended address.

Bars and Cafés

Cafetería Paradiso – *Rúa do Vilar, 29 – ☎ 981 58 33 94 – Open 8am-2am.* A café with a 19C atmosphere.

Café Derby Bar – *Rúa das Orfas, 29 – ☎ 981 58 59 04.* A timeless bar said to have been popular with the writer Valle Inclán.

Café Literario – *Plaza de la Quintana.* A stylishly decorated café with a young clientele, located at the top of a flight of steps with a fine view of both the square and the cathedral.

Vinatería Don Pinario – *Plazuela de San Martín.* A combination of interesting decor and a good selection of wines in this delightful square.

Index

A

Antiguo Colegio
dos Irlandeses — 51
Antiguo Hospital
de San Roque — 58
Aquariumgalicia — 106
Arco de Mazarelos — 55
Auditorio de Galicia — 69
Ayuntamiento — 49

B

Baiona — 111
Betanzos — 97

C

Cabo Finisterre/Fisterra — 99
Camariñas — 99
Cambados — 105
Cambre — 79
Casa da Conga — 52
Casa das Pomas — 52
Casa de la Parra — 52
Casa del Cabildo — 52
Casa do Deán — 52
Casa-Museo da Troia — 58
Casa-Pazo de Vaamonde — 51
Casa-Pazo dos Fonseca — 51
Castro, Rosalía de — 105
Cathedral — 40
Cedeira — 97
Cela (Camilo José) — 105
Celanova — 88
Centro Galego
de Arte Contemporánea — 65
Clavijo *La Rioja* — 19
Colegiata de
Santa María del Sar — 68
Colegio das Orfas — 52
Colegio de Fonseca — 50
Colegio de San Clemente — 68
Colegio de San Jerónimo — 49
Combarro — 107
Convento da Ensinanza — 55
Convento de Belvís — 55
Convento de las
Madres Mercedarias — 55
Convento de San Agustín — 56
Convento de San Francisco — 60
Convento de Santa Clara — 60
Convento del Carmen — 60

Convento del Colegio
da Compañía de María — 55
Corcubión — 99
A Coruña — 74, 75, 77, 79
La Coruña — 74
Costa de la Muerte — 99

F

Faculdad de Medicina — 60
Ferrol — 97
Fundación Eugenio Granell — 67

G

A Garda — 113
Gargantas del Sil (Gorges) — 88
Gelmírez, Diego — 14
O Grove — 106
La Guarda — 113

H

Hío — 107
Hostal de los
Reyes Católicos — 48

I

Iglesia das Animas — 57
Iglesia das Orfas — 52
Iglesia de la Compañía — 54
Iglesia de las
Madres Mercedarias — 55
Iglesia de O Pilar — 68
Iglesia de San Agustín — 56
Iglesia de San Benito
del Campo — 57
Iglesia de San Fiz
de Solovio — 55
Iglesia de San Fructuoso — 49
Iglesia de San Miguel
Dos Agros — 58
Iglesia de San Roque — 58
Iglesia de Santa María
de Conxo — 69
Iglesia de Santa María
del Camino — 56
Iglesia de Santa María
Salomé — 51
Iglesia de Santa Susana — 68
Invincible Armada — 74
Iria Flavia — 105
Islas Cíes — 111

L

Lugo — 80

M

Malpica de Bergantiños 99
Marín 107
Mateo (Maestro) 41
Mirador de Coto Redondo
  (Belvedere) 93
Mirador de la Curota 104
Mirador de Lobeira 105
Mirador la Madroa 111
Monasterio de Armenteira 107
Monasterio de San Estevo
  de Ribas de Sil 88
Monasterio de
  San Martín Pinario 58
Monasterio de San Paio
  de Antealtares 53
Monasterio de Santa María
  de Conxo 69
Monasterio de Santa María
  la Real de Oseira 87
Mondoñedo 95
Monte de Santa Tecla 113
Muros 104
Ría de Muros y Noia 104
Museo das Peregrinacions 65
Museo de Arte Sacra 66
Museo de Terra Santa 66
Museo do Pobo Galego 64

N

Noia 104

O

Oia 113
Orense 84
Ortigueira 96
Ourense 84, 85

P

Padrón 71, 104
Palacio de Amarante 58
Palacio de Bendaña 50
Palacio de Feijoo 56
Palacio de Fondevila 57
Palacio de Rajoy 49
Palacio de Santa Cruz 52
Palacio Gelmírez 48
Pazo Ramirás 51
Panxón 111
Parque de la Alameda 68
Parque Nacional de las Islas
  Atlánticas de Galicia 111
Pastor Díaz (Nicomedes) 96
Pazo de Amarante 58
Pazo de Bendaña 50

Pazo de Feijoo 56
Pazo de Oca 70
Pazo de Raxoi 49
Pazo de San Lourenzo
  de Trasouto 69
Pazo de Santa Cruz 52
Pazo de Santa Cruz
  de Ribadulla 70
Pazo Ramirás 51
Pico Sacro 70
Pinzón, Martín Alonso 112
Pita, María 74
Playa América 111
Plaza de la Quintana 52
Plaza del Obradoiro 48
Ponte Maceira 71
Pontevedra 90

R

Ría de Arousa 104
Ría de Cedeira 96
Rïa de Ferrol 97
Ría de Foz 95
Ría de Pontevedra 107
Ría de Ribadeo 94
Ría de Santa María
  de Ortigueira 96
Ría de Vigo 107
Ria de Viveiro 96
Rías Altas 94
Rías Bajas 100
Ribeira 104
Rúa do Franco 50
Rúa do Vilar 52
Rúa Nova 51

S

Santa Eulalia de Bóveda 83
Santuario de A Escravitude 105
Sanxenxo 107
Sarmiento, Pedro 91
Spanish Armada 74
St James, Way of 20

T

A Toxa 106
Tui 116
Tuy 116

U

University 54

V

Vigo 110
Vilagarcía de Arousa 105
Viveiro *Lugo* 96

Director	David Brabis
Series Editor	Ana González
Editorial team	Jeremy Kerrison, Alison Hughes
Picture Editor	Christine Chovet, Alexandra Rosina
Mapping	Michèle Cana, Daniel Duguay
Graphics and typesetting coordinator	Marc Pinard
Graphics	Jean-Luc Cannet
Typesetting	NORD COMPO
Production	Renaud Leblanc
Marketing	Ellie Danby
Sales	John Lewis (UK), Robin Bird (USA)
Public Relations	Gonzague de Jarnac, Paul Cordle

Manufacture Française des Pneumatiques MICHELIN
Société en commandite par actions au capital de 304 000 000 €
Place des Carmes-Déchaux - 63000 Clermont-Ferrand (France)
R.C.S. Clermont-Fd B 855 200 507

© Michelin et Cie, Propriétaires-éditeurs
Dépôt légal mai 2005 - ISBN 2-06-711545-6
Printed in France 04-05/1.1

No part of this publication may be reproduced in any form
without the prior permission of the publisher.

Typesetting: NORD COMPO, Villeneuve-d'Ascq (France)
Printing-binding: POLLINA, Luçon (France) - L97203

MICHELIN TRAVEL PUBLICATIONS
Hannay House - 39 Clarendon Road - WATFORD, WD17 1JA
☎ 01923 205240 - Fax 01923 205241
www.ViaMichelin.com - TheGreenGuide-uk@uk.michelin.com